The Eye of Love

In the Temple Sculpture of India

The Eye
of Love

In the Temple
Sculpture of India

Richard Lannoy
with drawings by Harry Baines

Hutchinson/Rider

Rider and Company
3 Fitzroy Square, London W1

An imprint of the Hutchinson Publishing Group

London Melbourne Sydney Auckland
Wellington Johannesburg and agencies
throughout the world

First published 1976
Text © Richard Lannoy 1976
Illustrations © Harry Baines 1976

Set in Monotype Baskerville

Printed in Great Britain by litho by
The Anchor Press Ltd and bound by
Wm Brendon & Son Ltd
both of Tiptree, Essex

ISBN 0 09 127760 4 (cased)
ISBN 0 09 127761 2 (paperback)

Contents

OVERLEAF:
*Khajuraho. Kandariyā-Māhadeva
Temple from the south*

1. Cults of Fertility

The profusion of temples nestling among stately trees gives the Indian countryside an ancient appearance. Passing through the doorway of a typical rural temple from brilliant sunlight to the mysterious dimness of the sanctuary, a pilgrim's eyes are drawn to little carvings on the threshold doorposts. Denuded of all superfluous detail by the hands of the devout, nevertheless one can instantly recognize images – at once both tender and simple – of lovers entwined in each other's arms. Medieval architects' manuals actually made it a rule that all temples must bear these *mithuna* sculptures on their doorways. It may be wondered what they mean. Unfortunately, no written explanation has come down to us, so, as with many details in this book, we must fall back upon interpretative conjecture. My explanation, however, cannot provide a clear-cut 'answer' to this question: why lovers on the doors?

They remind me at once of the two lovers in the Tarot pack. There they stand, tenderly embracing – yet so much more intimately and feelingly than our stilted Western pair! They entwine their limbs as if upon the very threshold of a new life together. Their love, these figures seem to be telling me, opens the doors of perception on an entirely fresh vista, a new way of looking at reality. In a moment they will pass from the ordinary light of day into another light, at the very spot where I myself take my first step through the door into the house of the gods. Doorways are, after all, *openings* – but on what images they open! Welcome, security, hesitation, temptation, desire, an unimaginable unknown.

In the third century A.D. Porphyrus wrote: 'A threshold is a sacred thing!' He meant that doorways are the boundary between two worlds, ordinary profane space and the sacred world beyond. Likewise, the threshold is the point where we pass from one mode of being to another, from one level of consciousness to another. To open the temple door recalls, perhaps, a moment when we ourselves open up to new depths of being. The most natural metaphor for opener and opening would surely be the dalliance of the amorous couple.

The feelings which inspired this custom of carving couples on temple doorways must first have been manifested very early in Indian history, in the formative centuries of settled agriculture. The rhythms and the routines of primitive cultivation were then seen as linked with the grand simplicities of birth, copulation and death. Everywhere for peasant populations settled in the vast alluvial plains, 'the myth of Heaven and Earth as a divine pair', MacCulloch pointed out, 'is the result of the analogy which man saw between the processes of conception and birth and those by which the earth brings forth. Hence in many languages the words for begetting, sowing and ploughing, for semen and the seed sown in the earth, for woman and the female organ of generation and the field or furrow, for the male organ and the ploughshare, are the same, or are used metaphorically one for the other. Hence Earth was regarded as fertilized by Heaven.'

A nameless Indian seer back in those remote times described the gate to the paradise of heavenly light as the very spot 'where sky and Earth embrace' (*Jaiminiya Upanishad Brahmana*). And in so far as a consecrated sacred spot on earth, a temple site, *becomes* the location of this cosmic event, so it follows that the temple represents the Cosmos, in which sky and earth are encompassed. Meanings begin to cross and interweave upon themselves, enriching the basic idea with complex associations. 'As above so below', goes the saying – and here they are, these amorous lovers, imitating the actions of the gods according to the immemorial pattern of all ritual. Like the myriad grains of pollen shed by the reproductive power in a single blossom, the marriage of Sky and Earth is re-enacted at every level: a divine coupling of deities, a regal marriage of king and queen, or simply the love of ordinary mortals.

Images of loving couples tenderly, playfully, or amorously entwined were extremely common in Indian sculptural art and have survived from as far back as the second century B.C. These sculptures are called *mithuna* in Sanskrit, that is a *pair* or *couple* or, more fully, the state of being a couple. But the earliest surviving sculptures to portray the sexual act as decoration outside or inside temples are to be found at Aihole, and date from the fifth century A.D. Explicit sculpted images of coitus fashioned in terracotta, but not forming part of the temple structure, precede these first erotic temple images by seven hundred years.

Mithuna. Buddhist stupa, Nagarjunakonda (in National Museum, New Delhi)

Such sculptures involving either copulation or genital foreplay are called in Sanskrit *maithuna,* or *copulation.* Between A.D. 500 and 900 maithunas are occasionally found, though neither very large nor very conspicuous, with a few rare and beautiful exceptions. For a final period from A.D. 900 to 1400 sexual representation became more and more frequent, more and more explicit, until we have a very high proportion of temple walls decorated all over their surfaces, exterior and interior, with sexual images. They vary in size from diminutive friezes only inches high to conspicuous life-size figures and groups, central to the temple's symbolic scheme. There are even several medieval temples *exclusively* covered with sculptures of maithuna. In this final and unprecedented flowering of sacred eroticism the couples are portrayed in every variety, pose and form of sexual play. The most prominent are placed on lotus plinths, a symbol otherwise exclusively reserved for sacred figures which are approached reverently, if not for worship. There are at least two dozen temple sites situated all over India from this final, medieval phase with fine erotic sculptures. Among these, the most famous, such

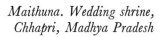
*Maithuna. Wedding shrine,
Chhapri, Madhya Pradesh*

as the temples at Khajuraho and Konarak, contain many hundreds of individual carvings of an explicitly sexual nature.

A few works, among which I would count examples illustrated here, are masterpieces of a high order. It would be a mistake, however, to consider these erotic sculptures as separate works, divorced from their context – which is always a temple. It is for this reason that we have chosen to illustrate this book with drawings rather than photographs. A documentary photograph tends to isolate sculpture, or to overdramatize detail at the expense of the whole, while a drawing can go beyond documentation to evoke the atmosphere of the temple. It is our hope that this evocative character of the graphic medium will help the reader imagine what it is like to step beyond the threshold and to experience a perceptible change in the way life may be viewed from the shrine.

Besides the immense surviving wealth of erotic sculpture and, no doubt, many times that quantity which has subsequently been destroyed by vandals, there are a host of humbler shrines peopled with quaintly appealing folk maithunas, products of less skilled village artisans.

India still retains primeval forms of worship, where the sacred is a volcanic, eruptive power. In his deeply thought book, *Eroticism,* Georges Bataille explains how 'at all times and in all places men have been fascinated and appalled by the notion of divinity. The words "divine" and "sacred" have carried undertones of an inner secret animation, a deep-seated frenzy, a violent laying hold of an object, consuming it like fire, leading it headlong to ruin.'

The sacred icons (*mūrti*) or cult images worshipped in the central shrine of many a pilgrim temple are another category of erotic image: male and female deities portrayed as displaying their sexual organs. Some are so lumpish as to appear subhuman, with swollen genitalia, gaping mouths, beady eyes staring from what looks like an amorphous mass of inflamed flesh or coagulations of semen. Many have been repeatedly coated with red oxide pigment. Such images are held so sacred as to draw pilgrims for hundreds of miles at annual festivals. They are placed in spectacular décor. To heighten the atmosphere, these images are generally 'dressed' in tawdry garments, or completely coated with the blackened grime of burnt offerings or the grease of clarified butter. Such cult images are venerated in every corner of the land, the most accessible and extensive surviving examples of ancient fertility cults.

The sacred is our name for the incandescence of life. At its very pinnacle, the sacred moment opens upon the abyss of violence or sexual paroxysm. We are then seized by two simultaneous emotions: a terror which would have us flee and a fascination which would consume us in the fire. Religion both imposes the tabu that maintains order as well as inspires its contrary – transgression. Such are the polarities which are the very life of religion; tabu and transgression are opposite sides of the sacred coin. Tabu forbids transgression but fascination breaks it. Images carved by those in touch with these primordial emotions within themselves reveal the passionate coalescence of their contrary pulls, the human yielding to blind frenzy. The thrill of transgression would be inconceivable without the very real power of the tabu; the permutations of these opposites are of inexhaustible variety.

I stress this fact here, as the element of the sacred as a sacrilege or transgression against society's deepest tabus is the very quick of Indian religion, its root and nerve. Its primeval imagery can and does co-exist with erotic art of ordered and lyrical refinement. Both figure prominently in the sacred cults, supported by the social prestige of the official, wealthy, establishment priesthood, the Brahmans.

With these deep strata of primitive Indian culture we reach the bedrock of our subject: the cultic association of sex with magic, or power. This is the climate of religious fascination with human sexuality, within which it was possible for a highly sophisticated and aristocratic art-form to grow. The early society in which sex thus plays a central role is tribal.

It is clear that India's cultic sexuality is immemorially ancient. The imagery of the erotic temple sculptures, a highly evolved art-form used by Hindus, Buddhists and Jains, is anterior to these religious differences, belongs to a kind of visual *lingua franca* that crosses doctrinal frontiers, and up to around A.D. 800 crossed regional, linguistic and geographic frontiers too. In the final medieval phase erotic imagery becomes regionally differentiated, but within the region is uniformly employed regardless of whether the temple is Hindu, Jain or Buddhist, whether it is dedicated to a male or female deity, and whether or not the official doctrine of the sect is of ascetic persuasion or its opposite. Maithunas were cultural property common to all Indian peoples, and an expression of an existential reality.

Each individual is born alone and dies alone. Between one person and another there is a vertiginous gulf that can be bridged by love, by mystical vorticism and by eroticism. The ecstasy of sexual rapture promises continuity of being, restoration in our raw and random individuality of that primal continuity. We so profoundly long to be released from our ego-capsule, to experience that state of being which links us with the all. The condition of man is to yearn for a flowing harmonious togetherness, a communion with others. Society is a partial reflection of this need; the social structure is obviously in tension with that impossible fluidity of communion for which the individual longs. In India the social structure is of a most intricate hierarchical composition and groups of people are hereditarily compartmentalized into castes. They must marry within the caste (and over ninety per cent still obstinately refuse to do otherwise). There are strict rules as to how castes relate to each other. This discontinuity, typically, is the direct opposite of the very union which our social instinct of togetherness seeks. Likewise, through religion man seeks to restore the lost continuity, the vanished unity of being, of oneness with the all. But, once again, we can see the tragic paradox of religions as comprehensive as India's. For, as in social organization, so in religious practice the curse of solitude is laid upon the individual. The Indian today lives in a state of encapsulated discontinuity. Socially he is condemned to an exclusive human group which cannot come into intimate communion with other groups. Spiritually, the Indian is very much on his own, seeking his encounter with the absolute deep within his solitude. At

Maithuna. Wedding shrine,
Chhapri, Madhya Pradesh

family level, husband and wife cannot even publicly display feelings of love and affection.

It would seem that it is our fate as a species to experience a division between the biological and the social, desire and duty, impulsive feeling and disciplined responsibility. In Indian custom, very great emphasis is given to the idea that sex is a hindrance to the attainment of self-realization, or enlightenment. In spite of an ascetic bias, Indian religion has always been thoroughly realistic in its recognition of human nature. Elaborate attention is given to the physical condition of the body. The very strict Hindu rules and tabus associated with eating, excreting, menstruation, bodily secretions and emissions are inspired by powerful emotions. The strength of the ascetic bias in Indian life is due to the almost overpowering force attributed to sexual desire in comparison with what is seen as a more fickle and feeble spiritual drive.

I have just referred to the polarity of the biological and the social as a perennial source of tension in all societies, resulting in varying degrees of alienation of the individual. India's efforts to deal with life's contraries always imply a surmounting of the opposites through a transcendent principle. The appetite for exalted self-transcending modes of concentration and ritual is exhaustively catered to in every Indian religious technology. Yoga, which we come to in a moment, is India's primary tool for self-reconciliation in the face of society's contrary pulls. Yoga itself rests upon a view of life as divided into a ceaseless play of opposites which resembles the well-known Chinese interplay of Yin and Yang, male and female principles. In India all religions hold in common the idea of two indivisible elements, a male and female principle, Purusha and Prakrti, Person and Nature, or Shiva and Shakti. The two elements originate in a single primordial being which manifests a 'desire to create'. From a unitary state of repose this emergent, but creative, tension gives birth to the universe and the multiplicity of beings and things of this world in a state of unceasing instability and flux, of time and constant change, of birth, reproduction, decay, death and rebirth. Out of a permanent coition of opposites the many are born, and with them confusion, antagonism, separateness. But the universe longs to regain its primordial state of oneness, and seeks to reverse the fragmentation. The return path, or restoration of lost unity, is the business of religion, yoga, ritualized sex, and its opposite: rigorous asceticism. These comprise a tool-kit of diverse, and divergent, religious techniques.

A single basic symbol expresses this interplay of masculine and

Lingam and Yoni. Rājgarh,
Madhya Pradesh

feminine principles: the yoni-lingam. Based upon the form of
vagina and phallus, this symbolic genital conjunction is one of the
commonest of all Indian cult objects. Less frequent are single images of
the yoni, or of the lingam. These images are highly stylized and
geometrical, an abstraction usually rendered in very hard stone.
They are sometimes clustered alongside temples in thousands; they
are still manufactured in millions. Their appearance, their cold,
obdurate, closed-in-upon-themselves density, suggests a meteorite
hurled at our planet from a stratosphere of remote, abstract, meta-
physical altitude. There is no other symbolic image in India as stark,
as unerotic, as the yoni-lingam. Some are of gigantic proportions.

Some are incised with a finely chiselled line, to indicate the male glans at the tip of the phallus; some have a snake coiled round the shaft, with its tail bedded in the trough of the yoni; some have one or more male human heads emerging from the shaft. In some temples there are whole avenues of the symbol. It is pre-eminently a product of the male mind and as such the epitome of the masculine Indian aspect of imagination.

Superficially, the phallic lingam signifies the human craving for immortality; more deeply, it is a symbol of creative autonomy, the root of force and singleness. For the worshipper of Shiva, the lingam is the sign of the transcendent. On the other hand, the yoni signifies not only the force of fertility, of birth-giving Nature, but the ceaseless play of appearances, the element of change in everything, every living being, all processes.

Together, as yoni-lingam, this image has numerous meanings: the conjunction of opposites, cosmic energy, union of male and female, interplay of masculine and feminine, dualism, monism, the root of being, a harmonious balance of gender. One thing it does not 'mean' is a copulatory conjunction of penis and vagina. A Hindu priest would object if one defined the lingam as a 'symbol of the penis'; on the contrary, he would define the penis as a symbol of the primordial lingam, a manifestation on the earthly plane of the supermale, cosmic energy. The proper place for the lingam in the cosmology of the Hindu temple is at its very centre, deep in the sanctum. Usually without illumination save for the entrance door, the shrine is generally unadorned. It is called the *Garbhagrha*, the womb-house, and in it this single stone looms from the silent shadows.

In spite of the prevalence of lingam symbolism, India is not at ease when the male principle is asserted to the total exclusion of the female principle. While the cultured, élite strains after an almost superhuman asceticism, invents portentous philosophical abstractions and has a male propensity for the impersonal, detached view, the average Indian is most relaxed and at ease only when the female principle holds sway. All the arts prefer the soft over the hard, and favour pliancy, curvature, sensuous delicacy of touch, portrayal of emotional states rather than the development of ideas. The sculptor, for example, shows a consistent preference for curvaceous, sensuous, juicy, succulent plant-like forms. It is not just that the arts of the temple are voluptuous, for so they are in the distinctly male-oriented civilization and art of ancient Greece. All evidence points towards an emotional preference of the aesthetic sensibility for everything pertaining to what Indians of both sexes intuitively feel to be feminine.

In contrast to the severely abstract lingam is the real feeling with which Indians carve or paint the profusion of lotus flowers covering entire surfaces and borders of their temples. The lotus flower is a symbolic substitute for the yoni, a cultic image used in association with various female deities, and signifies a visual analogy in Nature to the vulva. Temples blossom with its myriad flowers. They are almost as effective in evoking the convulsive, rippling coalescence of erotic rapture as are the maithunas which they border.

Much less abstract than the yoni-lingam is the couple who stand for a similar conjunction of life's basic opposites: Shiva as Prakasha, the 'first radiance', holds his spouse Vimarsha, reflection of his radiance, on his knee. The tendency to relegate the female of the primordial pair to the status of 'consort' is typical of medieval India, but not by any means universal.

Village India has enjoyed unbroken continuity in the expression of its deepest cultural traits for five thousand years. Mesolithic and neolithic artefacts are essentially no different from the products of craftsmen fashioned in clay for village fairs and folk festivals today, or the folk paintings which decorate village huts. Prominent among these simple images and objects are goddesses of fertility hardly differing in their smallest detail from those recently unearthed by archaeologists. As with such artefacts all over the world, the attributes of female fertility are greatly emphasized, such as prominent breasts, buttocks and thighs. The millions of rustic shrines scattered in profusion up and down the land, in every corner of the landscape, feature more images of female deities than male. In a population of peasant farmers, women play a more critical share in the labour involved. This, in part, accounts for the cardinal significance accorded to female deities. As far back as we can reach into the past this has been so, in spite of efforts made to glorify great male divinities in certain communities and kingdoms of patriarchal bias. In his excellent study, *Folk Origins of Indian Art,* Curt Maury explains how, to the vast majority of ordinary Indian people, the feminine principle is equated with nature. When personified as the lotus goddess, though she bore countless different names, she was really one – and only one – divine sovereign being. 'Regarded, not as the creative or sovereign ruler of nature, but as nature personified, the lotus goddess implicitly assumed the aspect of every one of nature's phenomena. The material universe was imbued with her essence. She indwelled earth itself and all living creatures that roamed it, every plant that grew from it, every spring and stream that fertilized it. Every cave that gave shelter was her domicile, every rock and stone a hallowed monument to her all-immanence. In the vastness of its diurnal blue and its nocturnal quietude the sky itself was the living mirror of her beauty, the luminaries and stars the habitats and dispensers of her powers, the elements but the reflection of her moods. Every particle of life was sacred: it was part of Nature, part of her own being.' Such an encompassing vision will inspire art very far removed indeed from furtive pornography or the anxiety-laden sensuality of Western eroticism.

One important feature of village culture almost always ignored by learned commentators on erotic Indian art is the uninhibited bawdiness of peasant humour and peasant sexuality. After all, the artisan castes and guilds – the great work-gangs employed to construct the temples, everyone actually involved in the building and decoration of temples – were all of low-caste peasant stock.

Viewed in the context of lofty Indian metaphysics and philosophy, such as we find in Sanskrit literature and scripture, the erotic sculpture is a perplexing contradiction, and commonly regarded by Brahmanically biased moderns as indecent. But viewed in the context of the daily lives of the rural peasantry there is nothing exceptional about it. Moreover, whatever moralistic judgement may be brought to bear on the subject, the sculpted themes are just as much a part of religious culture as the great mythical themes of classical Indian art. It is true that official, conventional or mainstream religion, as it is commonly conceived in India today, represented for two thousand years by Brahman orthodoxy, emphasizes the ideals of austerity, detachment, and renunciation. But this is a class-bound, very narrow view of Indian religion as a whole. For the majority of Indians – who happen to be the rural masses – these are very remote ideals. For the peasant it is idol worship and the seasonal festivals which count, and through which spontaneous feeling (and deep emotion) for all the primordial and most pressing concerns of life are expressed.

The festive calendar of rural India, with its frequent outbursts of saturnalia in the great seasonal festivals such as Holī, is the occasion when the religious feeling of the masses also presents socially legitimized occasions for the release of pent-up sexual feeling. At such times, too, the temples which most of the year are places of retreat, suddenly spring to life. They become the axis round which a seething mass of people are seized with collective frenzy. It is at such times that the carvings on the temple walls bear some visible relationship, in the quality of their earthiness, frank sexuality and their rhythmical exuberance, to the actualities of peasant life. For the reader to empathize from an armchair with the sacred frenzy of an Indian village festival may well be hard. I remember my own first contact with it when I was living in a village not far from the Ajantā caves. One day I heard a lot of noise, went to ascertain what it was, and found myself swept into a maelstrom of frenzied villagers surging across the fields to a small shrine. In all probability most of the crowd were either drunk on alcohol or *bhang* (a liquid concoction of cannabis), and the chief participants were in a state of glazed trance. Dancing, gymnastics, wrestling bouts, chanting, oracular possession, were followed by feasting. The drums never stopped for a minute, and all conventions were abandoned in the mind-numbing din. A kind of torrential incandescence possessed the throng, and at the centre of the vortex was an idol – liberally bathed in oils, fluids, pastes and powders. I have participated in a good many such occasions subsequently, and I know enough now to view Indian religion in a light very far removed from the discursive, unemotional, intellectual stance that one adopts, for example, when reading the great classical scriptures and works which expound orthodox Hindu doctrine.

I mention this because everything real and actual in any meaningful sense concerning the living stream of Indian religion can only be understood from a viewpoint of receptivity that is participative. This is just as true concerning appreciation of temple sculpture. Our persistently conceptual Western perspective, which locates the work of art outside the space and time of our experience, situating it in an ideal space, makes it possible for the spectator to look at it coldly from a distance. For the Indian mode of aesthetic involvement, the work of art is vibrantly alive, not a representation but a *presentation*, the word being *darshan* – which means the tangible aura of blessed *presence*. Sculpture begs to be felt, touched, fondled, smeared, bathed, polished. For the moment of identification, it is seen as if it were briefly the only existent thing, unique, desirable, intimately here, simultaneously now and always.

Hardly surprising, then, that one should frequently find that the genitals, pudenda and breasts of statues lovingly fondled by so many generations, incense burnt in clefts, protuberances smeared with oil, are permanently blackened. Worshippers will lick a finger and touch the pudenda of the female deities 'for luck', so that a deep touch-hole has been worn away in the stone. The touch-hole of one such sculpture in the Ellorā caves has been cemented over because some busybody considered this patina of devotion an obscene disfigurement. Devotees pass their hands over a deity, then stroke themselves and their children as if they were collecting and dispersing an emanation from the deity. Their lovely hands linger on the stones, not lasciviously but affectionately, with the ease of family intimacy. Sexual contact with the temple courtesan or *devadāsī* was another way in which the sacred was dispersed to the devotee.

Between the cult images of the folk and the highly refined master-works on famous temples there is a link deeper than difference in style would suggest. Both are rooted in a way of looking at life, a way of feeling, very far removed from the morose, furtive, male mastur-bative fantasies of modern pornography. We are a long distance, out here in the wilds of village India, from porn shops, blue movies, pin-ups, and leering male voyeurism or machismo. We call the earliest figurines made by man of the female figure 'Venuses'. The folk maithunas are continuous with that sensibility of early man who made little statuettes for finger fondling. The sculptors of Khajuraho and Konarak came from villages where the folk mai-thunas were familiar objects of daily life, objects associated not with debauchery and brothels, not with smutty stories or solitary mastur-bation, but with the home, with annual festivals, with rituals celebrating, affirming, and revivifying the well-being of the entire community.

2. Religious Eroticism

Indian temple art is almost consistently erotic and this eroticism has a sacramental character which in the Western world seems almost to constitute a contradiction. We are not in the habit of regarding sex as sacramental so I will try to define what I mean by 'religious eroticism'.

I take as my starting point the simple definition of Georges Bataille: 'Human sexual activity is not necessarily erotic, but erotic it is whenever it is not rudimentary and purely animal.' Unique among all species, man accomplishes a cultural transformation of sexual activity into eroticism. From simple sexual activity, engaged in for purposes of reproduction and the birth of children, we human beings have evolved a psychological and poetic quest independent of the original biological goal.

It is usually thought that the development of more or less constant sexual receptivity in the female of our species, a unique feature in the animal world, occurred because it strengthened the emotional attachment between males and females. Hence the father would be likely to favour mother and offspring in distributing foraged food. The urge to reproduce would, on its own, not suffice to ensure the stability necessary for the exceptionally lengthy nurturing of our species. Eroticism is evolution's answer; Eros is, so to speak, our social glue.

Not mere reproduction by copulation, but the culture of sex – that is one of our several distinguishing marks as a species, as momentous and indispensable as the development of consciousness, language, and the use of tools. The high mental development of human consciousness requires prolonged learning, rather than merely the hereditary transmission of animal instincts. Eroticism and consciousness are therefore deeply linked.

Even so, the sheer strength and limitless capacity for disorder, violence and promiscuity inherent in the human sexual instinct necessitates, at the dawn of our evolution as a species, the impo-sition on it of checks and tabus. These are amorphous and indefinable; all mankind observes them, but they are as varied as are human cultures. The tabu in Indian society against complete sexual liberty is as strong, if not more so, than in the Western world; its particular prohibitions – such as an overt physical expression of sexual attraction in public or even on physical expression among adults of feelings of affection and tenderness – are very strict.

Yet Indian culture, especially temple art, indicates that the whole capacity for sexual ecstasy of a peculiarly intense and sacramental form, is accessible to, and well understood by, a wide public, and has been so for a long period in its history. Modern puritanism clamped down on erotic culture several centuries ago, but there are still many people for whom sexual ecstasy is an inseparable feature of their religious life. As everywhere in the world, however, Indians view sexuality as a highly questionable phenomenon, an extreme form of experience that must be tamed and domesticated. While they show a deeper and more relaxed acceptance of religious eroticism, their social life is ringed with a very dense thicket indeed of protective customs which severely regulate its expression. In the West, religious eroticism may of course be found, but it is inaccessible to most people, who do not experience so unsettling a pitch of rapture in their conjugal relations. For us, the volcanic depths of eroticism are viewed as demonic, are even cultivated demonically, as in the oscillating, but frequent, phases of fascination with witchcraft, even in the middle of the twentieth century.

The product of Indian sacramental sexuality which is the subject of this book is art which portrays sexual activity of a remarkably gentle kind. Most erotic temple sculptures depict men and women suffused with sweet tenderness, never in the grip of violent delirium or frenzied paroxysm. The sculptor's is an act of restitution whereby the violence of transgression is surpassed rather than evaded, through evocative reference to sexual behaviour modified by religious training. An explanation of this training will follow shortly.

We call temple sculpture 'art'; by that we do not mean a private, élite form of solitary self-expression to be bought or shared with other members of that élite, but the expression of a whole community engaged in a common activity. This activity has religious aims and presupposes the existence of a relatively passive, never fully initiated laity, that is regularly convoked to attend festivals and rituals where they watch, listen, read or look – and then disperse. The temple arts solicit total attention, provide a 'total experience' which implies the attainment thereby of an absolute state of being described by the great religious mystics in scripture, myth and poetry. The quality of attention expected of the spectator-worshipper entails self-forgetfulness which dissolves the sense of an experiencer in the same way as does yoga. Keats addresses hīs Grecian urn, 'Thou, silent form, dost tease us out of thought, As doth eternity.'

The quality of paradisal innocence is very marked in all the best erotic Indian sculptures. I am reminded of the Christian mystic, Jacob Boehme, who believed that Adam spoke a language different from all known languages. He called this 'sensual speech', a language of the senses, proper to beings integrally part of nature. Indian musical theory claims the same thing: in origin, music derives from the 'sensual speech' of animals. Indian sculpture employs an intricate vocabulary of gesture. Thus, for example, on the Rājārānī temple at Bhuvaneshwar, Orissa, the female partner in some maithunas makes with her right hand a gesture of *abhaya mudrā*, gesture of fearlessness and assurance.

Most striking in these sculptures is the absence of any pornographic intention. Susan Sontag defines pornography as 'the representation of the fantasies of infantile sexual life, these fantasies having been edited by the more skilled, less innocent consciousness of the masturbatory adolescent, for purchase by so-called adults'. She spots a persistent emotional flatness in Western pornography that is due neither to a failure of artistry nor to unfeeling inhumanity, but is deliberately employed so as not to hinder the sexual response of the viewer. 'Only in the absence of directly stated emotions can the reader of pornography find room for his own responses.'

The innocent, untainted 'sensual speech' which the Indian artist aims for, highly coloured as it is with his own emotional feelings, is altogether a most unusual and rare thing to be found in the portrayal of the rapturous convulsion of erotic activity. From the viewpoint of society, convulsive sexual rapture appears contrary to our own dignity. 'The whole business of eroticism', Bataille rightly says, 'is to destroy the self-contained character of the participators as they are in their normal lives . . . the essence of eroticism is to be found in the inextricable confusion of sexual pleasure and tabu. . . . Stripping naked is the decisive action.' The idea of carving life-size monumental sculptures of people having sexual intercourse might strike some as sacrilege. If you come to think of it, this is not because an image will 'cheapen' a sacred, private act, for otherwise how would we tolerate images of breast-feeding, eating, or moments of ecstatic response to Nature? No, the visual depiction of sexual intercourse is normally a tabu in all cultures under most, but not all, conditions because intercourse itself is a convulsion, a turning inside out and upside down, a rending, a dissolving of self-possession. In Bataille's vivid phrase, 'bodies open out to a state of continuity through secret channels that give us a feeling of obscenity. Obscenity is our name for the uneasiness which upsets the physical state associated with self-possession, with the possession of a recognized and stable individuality. Through the activity of organs in a flow of coalescence and renewal, like the ebb and flow of waves surging into one another, the self is dispossessed, and so completely that most creatures in a state of nakedness, for nakedness is a symbol of this dispossession and heralds it, will hide. . . .'

It is evident that the sculptures illustrated in this book, although completely explicit in their depiction of genital activity, are not, in any ordinary sense of the word, 'obscene'. In fact, texts contemporaneous with the carving of the medieval sculptures state that the erotic imagery should inspire *drishti-shuddhi*, purity of look – the innocent eye, purged of anxiety, prurience or lust. Through our immediate, involuntary identification with the couples, their actions make the world transparent. They open us to that full and limitless state of being in which flowing continuity with everything is restored. For a moment we *are* the couple, we momentarily slip into a state of other-mindedness which is not the same thing as erotic arousal, as in pornography. The fundamental continuity, the flowing coalescence of all things, washes over us like the waves of a warm ocean.

Through the carved stones we learn that eroticism is one aspect of our inner life. The outward object of our erotic craving, the partner, answers the *innerness* of the desire. Eroticism calls inner life into play. This we often forget because sexual activity has an almost over-whelmingly explosive quality, of organs convulsively seething, of cravings that can lead to madness, a quality of something about to burst. Life around us, the media, advertising, small talk, push us ever nearer the brink of a contagious inflammation that, these ulterior stimulators would have us believe, can have its release only by recourse to some *outward otherness*.

Contemplation of the temple sculptures yields us to our innerness, separates us from everybody else, and invites us on a solitary quest for stillness, rather than the convulsion of ecstatic togetherness. The erotic imagery, curiously enough as it may at first seem, not only

OPPOSITE: *Chitragupta Temple,*
Khajuraho

gently impels us into experience of our innerness, into a kind of reflective glow, it also impels us into the sanctuary of the temple shrine. Now an Indian temple is not, like church or synagogue, a congregational shelter for worship in common with many others. The shrine is small, mysterious, a dark paradigm of the self in communion with the sacred. The loving couples on its outside walls instil a sensation in the worshipper of brimming fullness. In order to perceive fullness, to register it, be calmed by it, one must refer to that acute sense of emptiness which marks it off, and for which the small hollow core of the temple itself provides a location. The worshipper 'seeks sanctuary'.

Sex cannot be regarded as a mere off-shoot detached from the main course of life, as it is in the minds of most people, without being seriously misrepresented. Erotic activity is one of the very few instances in human experience that contain the potential for attaining the pinnacle of being. But descriptive language of any kind – words, poetry, paintings, sculptures, music – becomes irrelevant precisely at the decisive moment when all search, all effort, is over-reached, and one 'supreme' moment, Bataille says with succinct exactness, 'follows these successive *apparitions*. In the hushed silence of that one moment, that moment of death, the unity of being is revealed through the intensity of those experiences in which truth stands clear of life and of its objects'. The shrine, the holy of holies, is at once sepulchre and womb of rebirth to a state of enhanced consciousness.

3. Cults of the Body

The sculptures which are represented in this book were carved over a period of a thousand years and, while we call their sculptors Indian, they lived in different kingdoms and empires, spoke different languages, held widely differing religious beliefs, and carved images of love-play for a number of purposes, some of these being difficult for us to understand at such remove from them. Yet I hope to show how, even if we take into account the remoteness of these artists from our own day, our own way of life, their concerns and ours are not so very dissimilar. Indeed we have much in common.

The ideals which inspired the sculptors of India to portray with unparalleled sensitivity and joy the relations of the sexes were based on experience – experience being, for them, more fundamental than intellectual understanding. And their experience taught them that the only way to live more abundantly is through what Ananda Coomaraswamy described as 'a perpetual uncalculated life in the present'. He was explaining a particular quality to which Indians aspire, which is known as *sahaja*, or effortless being.

To understand the ideals which permit Indian society to embellish its most sacred shrines with images representing the erotic embrace, we must define the significance of that spiritual goal to which Indian religion is dedicated. This is most simply stated by Coomaraswamy as being 'the spiritual freedom which is called the ultimate purpose, the only true meaning of life, and by hypothesis the highest good and perfection of our nature'. More specifically, those temples which give special emphasis to sexual representation imply that liberation is unattainable without a partner who is of the opposite sex – in order to be oneself, to realize self-hood. There are many names for the state of being which we call 'liberation': moksha, mukti, nirvikalpa samādhi, sahaja, nirvāṇa. The Buddha was so named because he *woke up* (budh). The place in which he found himself upon waking from the dream of ignorance is described as 'the harbour of refuge, the cool cave, the island amidst the floods, the place of bliss, emancipation, liberation, safety, tranquillity, the home of ease, the calm, the end of suffering, the medicine for all evil, the unshaken, the ambrosia, the immaterial, the imperishable, the abiding, the further shore, the unending, the bliss of effort, the supreme joy, the ineffable, the holy city. . . .' The temples are to this goal what a child's scale-model is to the railway train – a replica of the delectably real. Some temples are models of the gods' paradise in the abode of the snow – the high Himalaya – or Indra's grove, or the World Mountain, or some again are models of the Cosmic Man. The Sun Temple of Konarak is a chariot of the gods, depicting all the joys of heaven, itself described as the 'realm of the sun', where reality is finally perceived as one boundless, formless, and timeless light.

'Yes,' the reader may say, 'that is all very well, but how do we attain this liberation? What about all the mumbo-jumbo of ritual, the foreign words, the philosophy?' I will try to show how the answer stays close at all times to the world of common experience. Wrapped up in the answer is a way of living which touches not only upon the whole field of sexuality, but on how we view the world, ourselves, and others, how we think, but more important, how we love and how we feel.

India's methods of attaining the goal of liberation are numerous. All come under the heading of *sādhanā*, a word for which we have no adequate English equivalent. Practice, discipline, training, personal growth, spiritual exercises of every sort – these are all sādhanā. To help others through work – that is sādhanā; to pray, meditate, perform rituals, practise yogic physical exercises – these too are sādhanā. The two most important kinds of sādhanā which will be mentioned here are: yoga and Tantra. Of these the more important is yoga.

'Only by yoga is yoga known' – goes the saying. Everybody has heard *about* yoga exercises – those strange postures that are supposed to be very difficult for the non-Indian. But yoga is really the basic mode of Indian religious concentration. It is non-sectarian, practised in all Indian religions. Primarily it is a way of viewing life, India's prime tool for achieving personal growth or self-actualization. Psychologically subtle, yoga can be viewed as an emotional therapy, even an emotional technology, ' . . . but we have nothing', writes Dr Alex Comfort, 'approaching the highly sophisticated technology for self-management and self-reconciliation to internal needs and those of the culture, which we see in "primitives".' The versatility, he says, of Hindu culture 'as an emotional tool-kit is staggering'. Yoga encompasses methods of personal growth which include techniques for rigorous and consistent asceticism as well as the attainment of ecstasy and enhanced consciousness through sexuality. This is not a contradiction or a confusion, for the irreducible basis of all yoga lies deeper than the specifics of its practice. Patañjali, the great ancient authority on yoga, who wrote the first and still the most authoritative yogic manual around the third century A.D., defined it as *citta vritti nirodha*, or roughly 'being aware without thinking'.

When we learn to drive a motor car we are faced with complex machinery, a set of pedals, a gear-lever, a wheel, and an instructor who tells us such things as: 'depress the clutch, engage first gear, depress the accelerator, bring the clutch slowly up to biting point . . .' and so forth. We look at the bewildering bits of machinery, we think about them, we try to remember what the instructor has said, and as soon as we bring the clutch up too fast we start to think about what to do next, the car jerks forward, stops, and the engine stalls. Where have we gone wrong? We *think* about it. We analyse our movements. By a very slow process we begin to coordinate the body with the mechanisms of the car, its movement and speed in relation to the road, and the traffic on the road. There comes a time when we are so totally absorbed 'in the current' of driving that we perform the manoeuvres without thinking: we proceed like a finger into a glove. That is as close as I can come to describing the process of yoga. It is a state less of 'concentration' that of total absorption – in experience. Of course, everyone 'experiences', but in the yogic way of experience, there is no experiencer, rather in the same way as there is no 'thought' as we change gear or alter direction while driving. Yoga is not 'presence of mind', it is *presence*. It is a silence of the prattling mind, the egoistic mind which tries to seize hold, to possess, to grasp, to dissect, to separate, to dominate or to coerce.

Yoga is like a man who, in the midst of crisis, remains calm, becomes detached – 'like a swimmer who remains dry'. The way of yoga is like the stillness of a pond; it is its own goal. Now, if yoga is the most basic way to liberation in India, if yoga is 'super-awareness' of reality, and is applied to everything we do, every second of our waking life, then it follows that yoga profoundly modifies the sexuality of a person who practises it wholeheartedly.

This is entirely consistent with a particularly emphatic importance given to body awareness. There is no culture in the world which enjoins such elaborate physical preparation for daily worship. For every aspect of sādhanā, or when embarking upon any spiritual experience, vigour and fine body tone must first be attained. It is not surprising then, that India regards the union of the sexes as the expression of the nature of Being. An example of this would be a tantric text like the *Vātula Shudda Āgama*, which states that the 'symbol of the vulva and the phallus represent the principles which cause the formation of the world. Their union expresses the nature of action.'

Let us see how yoga changes our whole approach to sexuality. It implies that the delight of sexuality is so fundamental that it cannot be reduced without attenuation of the nervous and somatic system. The force this pleasure means can only be *transformed*. Sexuality, for the yogin, is a new, genial, reorganization of the vital force – towards an object, or a fulfilment, more subtle or intense, larger or more immediate than an enhancement of consciousness and joy, if it is purely and transparently incidental to a rich and powerful art of experience. No 'art of love' can achieve this, only a centring of awareness. It can begin, of course, only when all fantasy has been conquered, and at first reduces all intoxication. Sexuality continues to be a moral or psychological problem so long as there is inhibition against sexuality as spontaneous, undifferentiated expression of affection and delight. Until innocence is regained the possibility of fulfilment of sexuality as an expression of richness and power, of primal energy, the energy of the whole person, is not in question and there can only be coercion, asceticism, perversity – inconclusive evasions, substitutions.

In other words, while there is still any fear of sexuality, any superstitious over- or cynical under-valuation of it – any sentimentality about it, any incapacity to accept it simply and wholeheartedly in all its possible modes, the question of sexual liberation does not arise. The yogic view makes it quite clear that to deny the Eros is to sterilize oneself, to kill or pervert all colour, iridescence, richness in one's conscious experience as a whole. For the Eros is the essential mode of transmission and modification of psychic energy and without erotic sensibility this flow and transmutation cannot long continue. The bell is tuned and purified by the vibration of other bells; this continual potentiality of reception and radiation sustains the field of sound as a prompt and subtle medium. It is so perhaps that Pythagoras may have felt the ceaseless sweet intercommunication of the stars, powerful, exalted, subtle chiming, ether that holds the rhythm of the Universe, instrument of 'the love which moves the sun and the other stars'.

There is one physical feature of yoga which visibly reveals its link with eroticism. I have already mentioned eroticism's convulsive

Purāṇa Mahādeo Temple,
Harṣagiri

quality, how bodies are opened out, turned inside out and upside down. Consider the 'lotus posture', basic position of the body in yogic repose: soles of the feet turned upwards, eyes rolled back to reveal the whites, breath arrested or at least slowed down appreciably. More spectacular examples are the convulsive churning movements of the stomach muscles. The experience accompanying these convulsions can be comparable in its intensity to erotic activity; in both we yield to innerness, given over to the tidal onrush of an oceanic feeling.

'Just as a man in the embrace of a beloved woman,' runs a famous passage from the Upanishads, 'knows nothing more of a without or a within, so also does the person, in the embrace of the knowing Self, forget everything that is without, everything that is within. This is a person's true form in which craving is satisfied, the Spirit and the whole of desire. This person has no craving any more, nor anguish.'

There are two main sources of information on Indian love-making available in written form: the classic sex manuals such as the celebrated *Kāma-Sūtra*, whose purpose is limited to instruction in the pleasures of love-making; and the more esoteric Tantra texts, where information on sexo-yogic rituals and techniques can be found. But the secret sexual lore is not to be found in books. More subtle features were passed on only by word of mouth from a guru to his or her disciples. Secret transmission of this kind is very common in every branch of knowledge in India, but is, of course, of particular importance in the subtle intricacies of sexo-yogic practices, since these vary greatly according to the stages of development and inclinations of individuals, or of couples. Before we look at the methods taught under a guru in the context of ritualized sexual intercourse, we should first look at the sex manuals, which are not in any specific sense associated with religion, but summarize India's basic approach to sex.

Vātsyāyana, author of the *Kāma-Sūtra*, made a synthesis of texts by former authorities on every conceivable aspect of the amorous arts. It achieved great fame and has been widely read by people wishing to be informed concerning the art of sex and the ways of the world.

The *Kāma-Sūtra* was written between the first and fourth centuries A.D. at a time when all the arts, not only sculpture, were becoming increasingly sensuous and extravagant in decoration. With pedantic thoroughness it classifies every type of lover and the appropriate permutations and combinations of sexual techniques, foreplay and coital postures suitable for these types. Vātsyāyana is a liberal with a very shrewd insight into human nature, sophisticated in so far as he recognizes a wide range of possible ways to approach sexual pleasure. But he is above all cunning and not averse to ducking moral issues by assuming a detached air to describe the stratagems of the seducer, the go-between, and the philanderer of both sexes. He oscillates between tiresome pseudo-scientific sententiousness and humour, all curiously familiar and modern. The *Kāma-Sūtra* and later manuals such as the *Ratirahasya* of Kokkoka, and the *Anaṅgaraṅga* of Kalyāṇamalla, all stress the man's responsibility for the pleasure and satisfaction of his partner. The *Kāma-Sūtra* is aristocratic in tone, and in the end leaves at least one reader a little impatient with its air of male *noblesse oblige*, redeemed somewhat by such congenial observations as have played no small part in endearing it to many readers: 'Of all the lovers of a girl, he only is her true husband who possesses the qualities that are liked by her, and such a husband only enjoys real superiority over her because he is the husband of love.'

The style of this love-making is very leisurely, balletic, and playful. Vātsyāyana's descriptions are highly picturesque. Here, for instance, he sets the scene for the ideal home of the cultivated man of the world:

This abode should be situated near some water, and divided into different compartments for different purposes. It should be surrounded by a garden, and also contain two rooms, an outer and an inner one. The inner room should be occupied by the females, while the outer room, balmy with rich perfumes, should contain a bed, soft, agreeable to the sight, covered with a clean white cloth, low in the middle part, having garlands and bunches of flowers upon it, and a canopy above it, and two pillows, one at the top, another at the bottom. There should be also a sort of couch besides, and at the head of this a sort of stool, on which should be placed the fragrant ointments for the night, as well as flowers, pots containing collyrium and other fragrant substances, things used for perfuming the mouth, and the bark of the common citron tree. Near the couch, on the ground, there should be a pot for spitting, a box containing ornaments, and also a lute hanging from a peg made from the tooth of an elephant, a board for drawing, a pot containing perfume, some books, and some garlands of the yellow amaranth flowers. Not far from the couch and on the ground, there should be a round seat, a toy cart, and a board for playing with dice; outside the outer room there should be cages of birds, and a separate place for spinning, carving and such like diversions. In the gardens there should be a whirling swing and a common swing, as also a bower of creepers covered with flowers, in which a raised parterre should be made for sitting.

The colourful prose of Vātsyāyana provides us with some parallels to the decorative setting, the luxuriantly carved niches and surrounding panels in which the erotic temple sculptures are placed. For example, here he describes 'Other Social Diversions':

Going out on moonlight nights. Keeping the festive day in honour of the spring. Plucking the sprouts and fruits of the mangoe trees. Eating the fibres of lotuses. Eating the tender ears of corn. Picnicking in the forests, when the trees get their new foliage. The Udakakashvedika or sporting in the water. Decorating each other with the flowers of some trees. Pelting each other with the flowers of the Kadamba tree, and many other sports which may either be known to the whole country, or may be peculiar to particular parts of it.

The *Kāma-Sūtra* is all for the prolongation of love-play; sexual congress should never be hurried, 'for if it takes a long time to allay a woman's desire, and during this time she is enjoying great pleasure, it is quite natural that she should wish for its continuation'.

Now some may ask here: If men and women are beings of the same kind, and are engaged in bringing about the same results, why should they have different works to do?

Vatsya says that this is so, because the ways of working as well as the consciousness of pleasure in men and women are different. The difference in the ways of working, by which men are the actors, and women are the persons acted upon, is owing to the nature of the male and the female, otherwise the actor would be sometimes the person acted upon, and vice versa. And from this difference in the consciousness of pleasure, for a man thinks, 'This woman is united with me,' and the woman thinks, 'I am united with this man.'

Here is Vātsyāyana the classifier:

There being nine kinds of union with regard to dimensions, force of passion, and time, respectively, by making combinations of them, innumerable kinds of union would be produced. Therefore in each particular kind of sexual union, men should use such means as they may think suitable for the occasion.

The commonest and favourite Indian metaphor for the seductive quality of a woman's movements in love-making is the creeper. Here are two variants of coital postures, described in distinctively Indian style:

When a woman, clinging to a man as a creeper twines round a tree, bends his head down to hers with the desire of kissing him and slightly makes the sound of sut sut, embraces him, and looks lovingly towards him, it is called an embrace like the 'twining of a creeper'.

When a woman, having placed one of her feet on the foot of her lover, and the other on one of his thighs, passes one of her arms round his back, and the other on his shoulders, makes slightly the sounds of singing and cooing, and wishes, as it were, to climb up to him in order to have a kiss, it is called an embrace like the 'climbing of a tree'.

Vātsyāyana puts much emphasis on amorous scratches and bites, and on the use of expressive sounds, for which there are fanciful names:

When a person presses the chin, the breasts, the lower lip, or the jaghana of another so softly that no scratch or mark is left, but only the hair on the body becomes erect from the touch of the nails, and the nails themselves make a sound, it is called a 'sounding or pressing with the nails'. . . . The lower lip is the place on which the 'hidden bite', the 'swollen bite', and the 'point' are made; again the 'swollen bite', and the 'coral and the jewel bite' are done on the cheek. Kissing, pressing with the nails, and biting are the ornaments of the left cheek, and when the word cheek is used it is to be understood as the left cheek. Both the 'line of points' and the 'line of jewels' are to be impressed on the throat, the arm pit, and the joints of the thighs; but the 'line of points' alone is to be impressed on the forehead and the thighs.

When the man, making the sound Phât, strikes the woman on the head, with the fingers of his hand a little contracted, it is called Prasritaka, which means striking with the fingers of the hand a little contracted. In this case the appropriate sounds are the cooing sound, the sound Phât, and the sound Phut in the interior of the mouth, and at the end of congress the sighing and weeping sounds. The sound Phât is an imitation of the sound of a bamboo being split, while the sound Phut is like the sound made by something falling into water. At all time when kissing and such like things are begun, the woman should give a reply with a hissing sound. During the excitement when the woman is not accustomed to striking, she continually utters words expressive of prohibition, sufficiently, or desire of liberation, as well as the words 'father', 'mother', intermingled with the sighing, weeping and thundering sounds. Towards the conclusion of the congress, the breasts, the jaghana, and the sides of the woman should be pressed with the open palms of the hand, with some force, until the end of it, and then sounds like those of the quail, or the goose should be made.

Obviously the participants in these charming rites of the love-bower must be refined and considerate people, well versed in the 'sixty-four arts' as Vātsyāyana calls the drawing-room skills of ancient Indian courtiers. 'Those who are possessed of excellent qualities are to be resorted to for the sake of love, and fame.' Such men are as follows:

Men of high birth, learned, with a good knowledge of the world, and doing the proper things at the proper times, poets, good story tellers, eloquent men, energetic men, skilled in various arts, far-seeing into the future, possessed of great minds, full of perseverance, of a firm devotion, free from anger, liberal, affectionate to their parents, and with a liking for all social gatherings, skilled in completing verses begun by others and in various other sports, free from all disease, possessed of a perfect body, strong, and not addicted to drinking, powerful in sexual enjoyment, sociable, showing love towards women and attracting their hearts to himself, but not entirely devoted to them, possessed of independent means of livelihood, free from envy, and last of all, free from suspicion.

The following are the ordinary qualities to be expected of all women:

To be possessed of intelligence, good disposition, and good manners; to be straightforward in behaviour, and to be grateful; to consider well the future before doing anything; to possess activity, to be of consistent behaviour, and to have a knowledge of the proper times and places for doing things; to speak always without meanness, loud laughter, malignity, anger, avarice, dullness, or stupidity, to have a knowledge of the *Kāma-Sūtra*, and to be skilled in all the arts connected with it.

To conclude this little anthology from the *Kāma-Sūtra*, here is Vātsyāyana relenting a little, allowing his readers plenty of leeway in how they follow his instructions:

About these things there cannot be either enumeration or any definite rule. Congress having once commenced, passion alone gives birth to all the acts of the parties.

Such passionate actions and amorous gesticulations or movements, which arise on the spur of the moment, and during sexual intercourse, cannot be defined, and are as irregular as dreams.

A man should therefore pay regard to the place, to the time, and to the practice which is to be carried out, as also as to whether it is agreeable to his nature and to himself, and then he may or may not practise these things according to circumstances. But after all, these things being done secretly, and the mind of the man being fickle, how can it be known what any person will do at any particular time and for any particular purpose?

The dance-like agility in which most of the finest carved representations of the love embrace are so carefully posed resembles the *Kāma-Sūtra* descriptions of coital postures. But we must now turn to an entirely different level of culture, the traditions of Tantra, for specifically sexo-yogic techniques. In order to do this, however, we must combine our investigation of techniques with those of a comprehensive sādhanā and a whole way of life – in its own way richer than that of the noble citizen who is the model for Vātsyāyana. Tantra, derived from the Sanskrit root, *tan*, to expand, means a system of techniques designed to achieve expansion of knowledge. Among these techniques are erotic ritual, poetry, speculative texts, painting and sculpture. The idea that the human body is a microcosm of something much larger – the universe – is essential to all Tantra culture. Based on a magical physiology of the body as the latter is experienced under special conditions induced by yoga, ritual, and sexual intercourse of a special kind, Tantra aims at the restoration

OPPOSITE: *Rajārāṇī Temple,*
Bhuvaneshwar

of unity in the split, divided, stress-laden, confused individual, and at the completion of a wholeness in which the presence of a partner to complete that whole is an absolute necessity. From the tantric point of view, the consummated human being is man and woman fused into one single unit. The body is not some 'thing' that a man or a woman has; a man *is* his body, a woman *is* her body. Tantra is concerned with the existent, not with fantasies or thoughts about what might or might not exist. Existence is identical with Being, or 'radiant light' as Buddhist tantrism calls it, an apt description of that state of animation, of sheer well-being when one is, simply, 'at one's best'. Thoughts, worries, fantasies, haunt us and eclipse the 'radiant light', abolish immediacy, 'now-ness' and leave us, so to speak, suspended in the anguish of *meanwhile*, the provisional, evasion, fear of the future, helpless anticipation. Thought is the mark of our fall from presence and from being 'lit up'.

Consider for a moment how you feel at a moment of peak experience. You feel a kind of contentment, you 'breathe easy' (a nice unconscious acknowledgement of yoga's emphasis on deep, sustained, tranquil breathing). The path of calculated resolve will not lead us to a state of 'radiant light'. If a person does reach it, he does so in spite of his calculations and in spite of his resolve. We slip unawares and unintentionally into such states. What is 'subtracted' is noise, the noise of thought, worries, busy-ness. Tantra calls such states Awareness. Life is suddenly as fresh as the dawn: we awaken to clear perception. Of course such states are unique neither to Tantra nor to Indian mysticism. An example that may be familiar to readers is the following, written in the seventeenth century by an English poet, Thomas Traherne:

The Corn was Orient and Immortal Wheat, which never should be reaped, nor was ever sown. I thought it had stood from Everlasting to Everlasting. The Dust and Stones of the Street were as precious as Gold. . . . The Green Trees when I saw them first through one of the Gates Transported and Ravished me; their Sweetness and unusual Beauty made my Heart to leap, and almost mad with Extasie, they were such strange and Wonderful things: The Men! O what Venerable and Reverend Creatures did the Aged seem! Immortal Cherubims! And Young Men Glittering and Sparkling Angels and Maids strange Seraphick Pieces of Life and Beauty! Boys and Girls Tumbling in the Street, and Playing, were moving Jewels. I knew not that they were Born or should Die. But all things abided Eternally as they were in their Proper Places. Eternity was Manifest in the Light of the Day, and something infinite Behind every thing appeared: which talked with my Expectation and moved my Desire. The Citie seemed to stand in Eden or to be Built in Heaven.

Traherne was recalling a state which, at least in childhood, we have surely all experienced. This state is the very contrary of need-centred love, that agonizing and seemingly insatiable quest for gratification. Fantasies and infatuations seem to exhaust our vital energy, our 'radiant light', and the body feels sour, depleted. The commonest source of heightened physical well-being is, of course, sexual delight. This is not only because sex involves pleasurable sensations. These are as nothing, can even seem poisonous, were it not for the togetherness of deeply shared emotions which suffuses the twosome whole, that melting together of the couple in which everything else in one's environment melts – in the warmth of closeness.

In so far as the goal is a unitary state of effortless Being, then the means to attain it imply a state of relatedness which extends to every aspect of our perception. The crux of this, for Tantra, is the attainment of a rapture so peaceful, so luminous, within the peak experience of sexual delight, that a melting union irradiates both partners with absolute 'impartiality' as to who is giving, who receiving, who surrendering, who experiencing. The 'we' becomes One, multiplicity becomes singleness. Here, implies Tantra, is a spontaneity which is naturally pure, non-dual: one's Being, in order that one may understand one's Being, manifests itself in the shape of man and woman. When one moves, a complementary movement is seen in the other. *There are no expectations*. A partnership flowers in value-cognition. What is real and unique in each is not veiled by interference in what is real and unique. No trace remains of ulterior motives to subvert or change 'for the better' what cannot be bettered. Love gives dignity to what there is. Tantra affirms and supports, seeks no proofs, asserts no prowess. It *begins* with sex, which is, after all, the beginning of ourselves. The deep interplay of maithuna-yoga generates a larger awareness that may transform carnal love, *kāma*, into *prema*, or undemanding love, and it is this which cleanses the doors of perception.

Tantra reveals a deep recognition of how conditioned we are to strife and striving, to mental games, to all the little subterfuges which Vātsyāyana so amusingly recounts and to which couples so readily resort – subterfuges of power, of coercion. Very little is written about how intercourse between couples should be performed. We know, however, that sexo-yogic technique is prolonged, and that this prolongation, if conducted in co-ordination with recitation of mantras, correct breathing, and with a kind of nimble mental sensitivity – which need plenty of practice – will lead to a qualitatively enhanced experience.

Rock-carved relief, Ellorā

For some reason as yet, it seems, unknown to medical science, sexual intercourse which does not involve copulatory movement but where the couple maintain a stillness of complete absorption in each other, accompanied by equally prolonged male erection possibly not even concluding with orgasm by either party, may attain a state of indescribable bliss, a melting and literally effulgent luminosity of a sweetness which surpasses that of 'normal' copulation concluding with mutual orgasm. This level of intensity may or may not be assisted by mantra, or with yogic breathing, or with yogic 'thought without thinking' in any structured, practised sense. It can even occur without any ritualistic element, quite spontaneously, as it were by accident – as long as the conjunction of the genitals is prolonged.

I see no point in describing tantric ritual here. It will not help us, I think, any more than the halting description just given, to evoke the quality of what is, in any case, not a matter of 'pure technique'. It is by no means infallible, were any one to follow such a course as I have indicated. Indeed, it would appear that there is a state, or a stage, where rules simply do not apply, technique is quite irrelevant and 'things just happen'. It will be obvious to the reader that if sexo-yogic maithuna is as motionless as indicated here, this hardly accords with the decidedly balletic, not to say acrobatic, character of so many Indian erotic sculptures. I have, however, indicated nothing as to what posture is advocated by the tantric guru. We know, for example, that Tantra does advocate the use of yogic postures during intercourse which require lengthy and arduous training. We also know that by around A.D. 600 there was a Buddhist sect, the Herūkas, whose members practised meditation during prolonged sexual connection, and that this was, and still is, performed in the Yab-Yum pose portrayed in Tibetan paintings and sculptures where the man either stands or squats, with the woman clasping her legs round the man's trunk in a squatting posture which aids motionless prolongation. The Yab-Yum pose is uncommon in erotic Indian sculpture.

This eroticism is not some kind of 'documentary' on sexual rituals. The sculptors were striving to portray a way of life, a system of values, a vision of an ideal condition. Such an aim is, surely, very hard to realize in art. But, as Goethe wisely said: 'only the inadequate is productive'.

4. A Cluster of Blossoms

The oldest erotic sculptures to have survived belong to a golden phase of Indian classical art when highly trained artists had not yet lost their links with folk culture. They are altogether devoid of that haunted tension between pleasures of the body and the joy of the spirit which so plagues the Western artist. These fragments from a remote age are not at all remote in feeling.

There never was before, nor since, a time in India like the flowering of the Buddhist kingdoms. In those days India was still under-populated, a vernal, fertile, unsullied land which permitted a fair degree of abundance and ease of cultivation. Kings acquired great wealth and lavished it with almost unrivalled prodigality on thriving cities and carefully tended parks. These garden cities were among the marvels of the ancient world. Greeks and Chinese alike were astounded by the splendour of it all. During the enchanted millennium of classical art the mood of India was, by comparison with the titanism and fervour of the Middle Ages, humanistic and illuminated by Buddhistic *metteya*, the 'sentiment friendly concord' But with each succeeding century sensuality became increasingly prominent. The mithuna couple had been content with a tender closeness to each other. Now the accuracy of erotic depiction reveals a more hectic determination to overcome at all costs the deadening effect of increasingly rigid social restrictions on the informality of spontaneous feelings.

My own first encounter with the great erotic sculptures was at Bādāmi. Here and at Aihole and Pattadakal, not far distant, the most monumental maithunas from the early phase in this kind of sexual representation are to be found. They were mostly carved in the sixth century A.D. in the reigns of the Chālukya kings, a feudal dynasty whose capital for a time was Bādāmi. This was the period of retrenchment in Indian history into a village-oriented and feudal

Flying couple. Aihole (in National Museum, New Delhi)

culture from the rich mercantile prosperity of the classical and Buddhist era, when the influence of spacious and cosmopolitan city culture lost its impetus. Bādāmi struck me as a peculiarly magical and unpretentious place, having relapsed back into rusticity, little more today than a village, but strewn with the remains of more kingly days, and thereby expressive of how tenuous is the hold of high civilization in a continent overwhelmingly agricultural. The very earth and rock of Bādāmi reveal the origin of its name, which means 'almond coloured' – for the orange and russet rock out of which its four splendid rock-cut cave sanctuaries are carved epitomize this consistent earthiness and physical quality that is never lost at any time, no matter what degree of refinement in workmanship may gloss it. One is completely surrounded by this insistently gritty and granular russet substance. The sculptures are massive, placid

OPPOSITE: *Rock-carved pillar, Bādāmi*

and sensuous. I saw it in the loveliest season, with flowering trees ablaze next to the intricately wrought verandah pillars. The sun bathed the warm-coloured rock, dappling its streaky veins of colour. I was steeped in an almond trance. Everything was bathed in light; even the shadows were liquid with light. The sculptures were as ripe fruit on the bough, succulent, juicy. The deities, with their splendidly physical well-being, *breathed*, as if the elements in this amalgam had been infused with life. The Bādāmi caves, carved with a pre-eminently sunny, loving tenderness, are fecund, vernal, terrestrial. On the pillars there are large and intricate capitals bearing a restrained, relaxed sequence of maithunas absorbed in the sweetness of genial love-play. I am not likely to forget the moment I realized that I was looking at sculptures portraying the most intimate sexual delight. The immediacy of the moment, the magic of it, was so unemphatic, so unstressed, that it had a quality like honey poured on honey.

The deities are distinctly regal in appearance. In this new feudal climate of India it was the king in whom were vested the responsibilities for ensuring that people's needs were met. These included

Kinnara couple. Shiva Temple, Aihole

food, the sun and rain which provide food, besides victory through skill and strength; unity, and unity on wise rules and obedience. The ritual of the temples was designed to secure all these good things, all that contributed to the full life.

A result was that the temple, while retaining its essentially sacred character was viewed, as it were, through the rose-tinted spectacles of the courtier. The assembled gods were modelled on the splendour of the courts, and the courts were modelled on the splendour of the gods who resided in their Himalayan palaces, or in Indra's grove on mount Sitānta full of rock and cave-houses. The temple, and the myths which are the subject of its sculpted panels, completes the desired identification of man and god for the attainment of plenty. Kings are divine, they are impersonations of gods, and as such have all the attributes of godhead, so that what is true of the god is true of the king and *vice versa*.

On the ceilings of the Bādāmi caves and Aihole temples are portrayed delicious flying couples, Gandharvas and Kinnaras, amorously interlaced in scalloped cloud penumbra and swirling vegetation. There is a story of how Damayanti, at a loss to distinguish her lover from the four gods who have assumed his form, in her distress prays to them to reveal their divinity. They do so by appearing 'sweatless, unwinking, crowned with fresh and dustless garlands, and not touching the ground'. This is a charming verbal equivalent to the weightless and unearthly – but not un-sensual – flying figures.

A feature of the erotic motifs at Bādāmi is the presence of attendants beside couples making love, bearing in their hands stringed instruments, fly whisks and jars of wine. One scene of a couple in close embrace shows an attendant standing by with the wine-jar, face averted, and in other scenes the attendants place their hands over their eyes. Later, at Khajuraho for instance, the attendants assist in love-making. These scenes closely parallel those in literature, notably such dramatists as Kālidāsa and Bhāravi, who are eulogized in an inscription at Aihole.

India never lets us forget that we are in the world. Through the body there is experienced the corporeality of things. A place as steeped in the physical as Bādāmi induces a change in the physical intensity of our bodies. This experience of and through materiality is a threshold to a much wider world than the merely tactile. Because we describe the threshold as opening on the 'beyond' that is no reason to believe there is a world other than we experience. The way we interlace with the world of nature, or our love partner, is based upon our possession of a body with uninterruptibly present bodily organs of perception. Tantra's name for my Bādāmi experience is 'radiant light', our capacity to experience increase or decrease in levels of luminosity. We relate to the images of love because they too radiate well-being; the visage of the lover is palpably shining with happiness – a marvellously felicitous rendering of the luminosity of Being as we experience it ourselves in moments when there is an absence of all obscurity. But to perceive that shining quality in an appreciative, discriminating, non-judgemental way there must be a congruence between our own state of receptivity and that imaged in the sculpture. I give it as simple a description as I can – all others are laboured reconstructions after the event: happiness of concentration. There is no question of 'thinking about', of 'analysis', and – horrors – 'critical assessment'. In retrospect, I have come to the conclusion that the gravely tender mood of the Bādāmi lovers derives from the fact that they are carved in the living rock of *caves*. They have a look of being drowned in stone, as if drifting in the unsounded depths of molten rock. They are barely more than awake in the dawn of a conscious erotic sādhanā. They still do little more than bask in a hypnogogic trance between dream and awakening. This mood is en-

*Dancers. Rock-carved Buddhist
ćaitya, Kārli*

tirely distinctive from the incandescent rapture of the lovers in the
high Middle Ages, who embellish the airier and more fretted towers
of constructed temples.

The dawn of erotic culture is slowly revealed, too, in the remarkable
mutations which successively occur in the sculptor's treatment of
vegetation. This can best be seen in the doorways of Ajantā cave
sanctuaries and the temple at Deogarh, where the love couples attain
a peak of perfection. The voluptuous mithuna statuary is carved with

Couple in a rocky landscape. Gateway, Buddhist stupa, Sānchī

a luxuriant sensuality of elegance, refinement and tenderness. The remarkable feature of these sculptures is the way in which the sap-laden vegetation curling and winding over the surface of the stone, and in which single male figures seem almost to *swim*, is itself a paradigm of sensuous physical well-being. I know of no art in the world quite like India's for the way foliage, creepers and flowers can evoke through fashioning human hands the quintessence of sexual delight, like the tracing of patterns on skin by caressing finger-tips. The creeper is very widely alluded to in sculpture and poetry. So closely is the creeper identified with female beauty as to be synonymous with it. A form of sexo-yogic maithuna is known as *latā-sādhanā*, *latā* meaning a vine or creeper. 'As the creeper embraces the tree on all sides, so do thou embrace me' (*Atharva Veda*). The goddess Gaurī is described as half of Shiva's body, 'embracing him as the Mādhava creeper clasps the Young Āmra tree with her bosom like a cluster of blossoms' (*Yogavāsiṣṭha*).

In response to this association of female sensuality with vegetation, the sculptors invented a hybrid plant, the lotus creeper, which entwines its sensuous, serpentine stalks and flowers profusely across the gates and doorways of shrines, curling around figures in a luxuriantly erotic embrace that is startlingly human. This was an age when the details of natural forms, plants and animals, were

Nāga king and queen. Rock-carved relief, Ajuntā

almost as important as figure sculpture.

But then, at the peak of classical skill, the lotus creeper and most details of nature disappear. They seem to have been absorbed into the bodies of the human figures, or, rather, the human figures assimilate the qualities of the vegetation. Bodies are portrayed as ivory-smooth, but details, such as hands, nostrils, lips, curls of hair, ear-lobes, toes, acquire a plant-like quality, and they resemble the sap-laden lotus creeper. Sarnath, the deer park where the Buddha had preached his first sermon centuries earlier, became the centre of this art, and here the figures are steeped in a dreamy inner sweetness, as if the feminine principle, hitherto located in the breathtaking freedom of nature's impossible sensuality, were suddenly internalized, rediscovered in the inner life of the psyche. Certainly, no figure more perfectly incarnates the state of sacred inner marriage, the bliss of nirvāṇa, than the famous Sarnath Buddha, a fifth-century masterpiece.

Now the interesting point about the facial type of Sarnath classicism is its ethnic affinity with tribal physiognomy. We find these round and placid features today only borne by Indians who are ethnically either tribal or very close to the ethnic strains of India's tribes, especially the lower-caste Hindus. This is important to our story, for the thread of ebullient eroticism in all subsequent Indian

Scroll pattern. Hoysala Temple

history never severs its connections with its tribal origins. The consistency with which sculptors preferred a canon of human beauty deriving from tribal physiognomy directly contradicts the high-caste and aristocratic canons of beauty, with a preference for the more angular features and aquiline nose of high-caste Aryan ancestry. In all subsequent periods, wherever erotic sculpture flowers in relaxed freedom, there too the tribal physiognomy will be the model type, the ideal of free and joyous sensuality.

Once sculptors had learned the trick of transforming the human body into a plant-like sinuosity, they had the formal means to portray erotic rapture in all its rhythmical and rippling pliancy. Stella Kramrisch called this 'transubstantiation', a way of expressing a metamorphosis comparable to the transubstantiation of the bread and wine into the body and blood of Christ. The bodies of man and woman can thus be seen yogically, as the incarnation of divinity in human form. Sexual intercourse becomes directly instrumental in attaining this divinity, or state of Being. With marvellous dexterity, the sculptor creates the impression that resistant stone, like resistant flesh, is infused with an inner sap, or vital fluid. Figures sway, curve, and entwine themselves round each other like creepers in the famous *tribhanga* pose, the triple curve. This later reaches its apogee at Khajuraho, where the temples are almost

OPPOSITE : *Rajārānī Temple,*
Bhuvaneshwar

entirely devoid of floral embellishment, but the couples form a bower of entwined limbs as sinuous and foliated as the sprouting luxuriance of decorative classical ornamentation. Once, and only once, the lotus creeper and the floral border re-emerge in an explosion of youthfulness and exuberance, around the lovers which cover the surface of the Sun Temple at Konarak.

I said a moment ago that the lotus creeper vanished within the bodies of Sarnath carvings. This is not quite so fanciful as it sounds. For you will see in a moment how, in tantric yoga, one can experience a gradual upsurging current of energy within the body which is described as passing through a serpentine stalk along the spinal column, 'flowering' successively in a series of *chakras*, or lotus-centres. The nearest carved approximation to what is a *sensation* rather than a physical modification of the inner organs of the body is the serpentine rhythms of the erotically animated couple. The artistry is such that we feel these invisible inner movements as a current of energy within the stone, and the lovers undulate in rhythm with the onrush of the releasing storm.

5. Tribal Origin of Tantra

The presence of sexual representation on temples in the early Indian medieval period coincides with the emergence of Tantra into the stream of Hindu culture – that is somewhere between the fourth and sixth centuries A.D.

It is commonly held that Tantra is of tribal origin. The basis of all Tantra – Hindu and Buddhist – is the performance of ritual sexual intercourse by a circle of couples who are not married. We will come to the tantric doctrines in a moment, but let us start by focussing on its tribal origins. I call this phase 'primitive Tantra', when it has little to distinguish it from tribal custom, except that it is practised by members of the caste society, by way of being an alternative system rather than in opposition to, or in protest against, social norms. It was almost certainly practised at first by the lower castes and was quickly adopted by the aristocracy, for which there is abundant evidence in every kind of cultural material of age-old, if unofficial, symbiosis, let alone the fact that the majority of all feudal Hindu dynasties are well known to have been of low-caste or tribal origin.

I believe that Tantra began simply as an orgiastic group-sex rite occasioned by seasonal fertility festivals, and subsequently went through the familiar process of incorporation into the mystical mainstream of Hindu and Buddhist religion, probably through the agency of men and women who were of tribal origin, but who had learnt to use yoga. Sooner or later, yoga and ritual orgiasticism were bound to coalesce. An obvious consequence in the practice of yoga is the toning up of the body in a way that enhances muscular suppleness, improved breathing and the sense of rhythm. Moreover, I have already tried to describe how yogic experience has a physical effect closely allied to orgasmic rapture.

The concept that semen is an energy-substance which, instead of its expenditure by emission, can be redirected upwards to be diffused throughout the body as a kind of radiance, is an ancient discovery of yoga. In Hindu Tantra the theory is that, with avoidance of male ejaculation in intercourse, re-circulation and subsequent transformation of the vital juices will induce bliss. It is this yogic technique adapted to *group* sex which is the germ of the whole complex known as Tantra. And I have a shrewd suspicion that the appeal of Tantra to the cultivated classes was, in part, derived from the reputation which its sexo-yogic techniques had for providing keen sexual pleasure and at the same time ensuring a measure of birth control.

To this end, the tantric gurus instituted the practice of the Shakta Chakrapuja, ritual intercourse by a circle of paired men and women, and this rite, all authorities are agreed, is the foundation of the tantric sādhanā.

The orgiastic scenes on temples contain one revealing detail which link them with tribal culture. As far as I know, this has not hitherto been noticed by commentators on erotic temple sculptures. This is the portrayal of hair-grooming in, or adjacent to, scenes of orgy (*see* opposite). Now, hair-grooming is obviously not wholly unknown in Hindu love-making. But it has nothing like the same significance as it has for the boy and girl, Chelik and Motiari, members of the 'kingdom of the young', as the Muria tribe calls the youth dormitory, or *ghotul*. For them, the combing of the boy's hair in the evening is a highly significant interlude invested with the gravity of ritual.

The ghotul, which survived in its fullest form among the Muria tribe, was nevertheless widespread in earlier times, possibly universal among India's large tribal population, and notably in regions adjacent to the areas where the erotic temple arts were carried to their peak. Dr Verrier Elwin, whose vivid eye-witness account of this institution is the subject of a book called *The Kingdom of the Young*, tells how 'Muria boys and girls are susceptible to tickling, which has been described as "the most intellectual mode of touch sensation and that with the closest connexion with the sexual sphere". As the motiari dresses her chelik's hair and with her comb gently tickles and stimulates his back and arms, he responds by fondling her breast, by stroking her legs (which are usually placed round his body; as she massages, the girl often grips the boy's waist between her knees) or by boldly tickling her. Certain types of massage are specially exciting. The girl stands above the boy, bending over him and rubs downwards, passing her hands over the stomach down to the specifically erogenous region which thus receives a powerful

Maithuna and hair-grooming.
Bagali, Bellary district,
Mysore

tonic; sometimes she massages the legs, pushing her hands right up to the groin.'

The outstanding feature of the ghotul is what ensues after the evening hair-grooming. The boys and girls, who number around twenty in each village ghotul, engage in dancing, singing and poetic recital, followed by sleeping together in pairs in the same room. In one type of dormitory, called the *jodidar,* or 'yoking' ghotul, writes the anthropologist Elwin, fidelity to a single partner is maintained during the whole pre-marital period, prior to their joining the adult society. The word 'jodi' is used of a lifelong friend or yoke-fellow. In the second type of ghotul any kind of lasting attachment between chelik and motiari is forbidden. Pairs sleep together for three days before there is a change in the circle. This is not a custom of licensed promiscuity, but, on the contrary, it develops very deep bonds between the inmates of the ghotul which last for six to eight years.

I believe this link between Tantra and ghotul is amply borne out by the ethos of the tribal life-style. Dr Elwin, himself married to a tribal woman, personally visited and stayed in over three hundred ghotuls in the late 1930s. What follows in quotation from his classic on the subject, seems to me to express most aptly and comprehensively a way of life wholly distinct from official, conventional, Brahmanical Hinduism, and yet again wholly distinct from the ethos of village India today. But many observers of the Indian scene, including the distinguished art historian, W. G. Archer, are of the opinion that tribal life as he and Elwin knew it in the 1930s and 1940s, was the last living reminder of Indian village life in the days when the erotic sculptures were carved.

It so happens that Elwin's description of these young Muria inmates of the ghotul can also serve as the best description I can find of the simple down-to-earth ethos of people close to the soil for whom and by whom these sculptures were carved. Elwin is particularly struck not so much by the degree of sexual freedom but by the quality of relationship on which it is based, and where 'everything is arranged to prevent long-drawn intense attachments, to eliminate jealousy and possessiveness, to deepen the sense of communal property and action. No chelik may regard a motiari as "his". There is no ghotul marriage, there are no ghotul partners. "Everyone belongs to everyone else." A chelik and motiari may sleep together for three nights; after that they are warned; if they persist they are punished. If a boy shows any signs of possessiveness for a particular girl, if his face falls when he sees her making love to someone else, if he gets annoyed at her sleeping with another chelik, should he be offended if she refuses to massage him and goes to someone else, he is forcibly reminded by his fellows that she is not his wife, he has no "right "over her, she is the "property" of the whole ghotul, and if he looks like that he will be punished. . . . The calm level of affection – almost as of mature experience – which they achieve while yet in their teens, expresses itself in the wonderful harmony and fellowship of the best ghotul, the general diffused affection which leaves no room for jealousy and possessiveness. As anyone who has stayed for a time in a good ghotul must notice, the boys and girls form a compact, loyal, friendly little republic; they are all evidently very fond of each other; there is a large, generous, corporate romance uniting them. They do really seem to live in a sort of glow; the superb light of cleopatrine passion is absent, but so is the harsher glare of excited grasping lust. In the soft diffused glow of corporate affection, a girl decorates herself not only for one boy, but for all the boys and for the ghotul's honour and delight. The boys drum and dance to please their special lovers, it is true, but also to excite and gratify the entire company of motiari. . . . Chelik and motiari are continually enjoying sexual congress in company; every night a boy can watch his neighbours if he wants to, he can show off his sexual prowess if he feels so inclined. Actually there is a strong tradition against "peeping", except on the night when the chelik shut up in a room the newly-married pair. Then they may listen and try to peep through cracks in the wall. . . . Chelik and motiari do, however, often sleep together without sexual congress. The girls have a practice, called dinga-dinga, of playing with the penis, and the great prominence given to the clitoris in drawings suggests that they indulge in some form of clitoridical stimulation. But full sexual intercourse is everywhere the rule, and is normal through all divergences and for every type of ghotul.'

I am not suggesting that the sex-life of the tantric circle is the same as that of the ghotul. Rather, I think it likely that tantric sexo-yogic rites are a nostalgic re-creation by caste Hindus of practices common among tribal forebears or tribal neighbours. One could assume, too, that tantric practices reflect the taste of a leisured ex-tribal court élite in search of novelty. Similarly, I am not suggesting that erotic temple sculpture depicts the love-life of chelik and motiari, but that their delicate and youthful idealism informed the lives of the sculptors at that period in certain areas of the interior where interaction between castes and tribes was particularly close. The development of tantric cults with elaborate secret rituals is something else again, calling for a more private art, of miniatures, for example, and aids to meditation among small groups such as diagrams and mandalas (which have survived in abundance), rather than a popular public art such as our great temples with their monumental erotic sculpture. It is the original source of tantric culture and erotic sculpture which is common to both. Subsequently, the prestige of the tantric sects assured an influence on temple art but not very much more than influence. Erotic sculpture is uncommon on the chief tantric shrines. It is a certain human atmosphere I want to evoke, because it was human feeling after all which was the original source of inspiration. That atmosphere could, until a few decades ago, still be directly experienced only in tribes whence came those earliest promptings of the heart to fire the temple artificer.

It will be clear from this description that the eroticism of the ghotul is entirely different from that described by Vātsyāyana in the *Kāma-Sūtra*, but is, at least in a physical sense, not so greatly unlike that enjoined upon the non-marital partners in the tantric rite of

maithuna. Conventional caste Hindus have always had a feeling of
contempt for the dark-skinned tribes. They fear their vigorous
extroversion and, as one would suspect, rather envy them their
easy-going ways, their spontaneous lyricism, and their lack of sexual
inhibitions. The tribes are the social antipodes of caste India *par
excellence*. At the same time, the Hindu builds a defensive fantasy
against them, calling them 'shiftless fellows', 'barbarians', 'drunks',
and because they eat meat, unclean, too.

Signs of the secrecy surrounding Tantra in the first four or five
centuries of its practice are apparent in the erotic sculpture of the
seventh and eighth centuries at Bhuvaneshwar and Puri, where the
images of maithuna are placed in inconspicuous, almost hidden
positions, whereas auspicious mithuna couples are very prominent
(as had been the custom for several centuries already). This difference
would suggest that by the seventh and eighth centuries the primitive tantric ethic as a way of life was losing ground to secret, or
esoteric sexo-yogic cults of a more fully articulated religious sort.
There is little to suggest thereafter that the gentle commune
tyricism of tribal love-life survived for long among those sections of
the caste society dominated by patriarchal Brahman orthodoxy. As
we might expect, this spontaneity survived among the temple

Lakshmaṇa Temple, Khajuraho

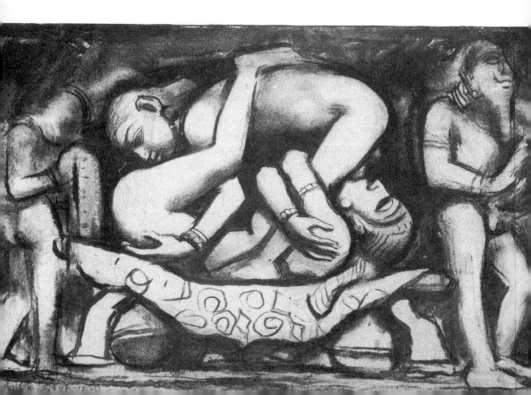

artificers – throughout Indian history of quite humble social origin. But this was the period when the caste regime became increasingly inflexible and rigid in its principle of stratified, exclusive groups, and esoteric secrecy was rife in the transmission of religious doctrine.

Tantra has something of the same protean quality as does the erotic imagery of all Indian religion, no matter by which sect or school it is used. Tantra is neither exclusively Hindu, nor exclusively Buddhist (tantric Buddhism is a major cultural phenomenon that lies outside the scope of this book), nor is it exclusively used by worshippers of the two main Hindu persuasions, the devotees of Shiva or of Krishna. It belongs to the deeper substratum common to all Indian religions, part of the cultural *lingua franca*.

Fully developed Tantra conceives reality as the interplay of the deities Shiva and Shakti, or the primordial male and female. It retains the central focus of Hinduism on the human body as the epitome or microcosm of the universe, and regards the body as a kind of temple, a living effigy of the universe, which contains all truth. Shiva and Shakti are felt to inhabit the body at its opposite extremes, Shiva in the thousand-petalled lotus, the Sahasrāra, and Shakti at the base of the spine, a dormant serpent power – kuṇḍalinī – coiled within the Mūlādhāra-chakra. Activated, the female energy

rises upwards through the body, a psychic energizing force rather like a comet passing through the heavens, and modifying the 'galaxies' of the chakras in its path, till it reaches the thousand-petalled lotus in the cranium. Through this union the body is radically modified, flooded with effulgent light and bathed in nectar. Through control of breath by yoga, and above all through control of seminal emission, the vital energy is brought to an enhanced state of harmony.

Around the sixth century A.D. we see the first portrayals of orgies (at least among those sculptures which have survived from so long ago), including oral-genital congress and congress from the rear. These become common in later centuries and are supposed, therefore, to refute the theory that erotic sculpture is associated with mystical, sexo-yogic ritual of Tantra, since oral sex and congress from the rear form no part in Tantra. Tantric rites do, nevertheless, involve couples having intercourse in a circle, presided over by their guru. I do not think this is by any means proof against the theory that the orgy scenes have no cultic association, though it is clear that they definitely are not yogic.

Portrayals of orgies on Indian temples are always quite small, mostly low down on the base lintel. Their figures are reduced to the status of diminutive cyphers. I take this as tacit recognition of the fact that the whole point of an orgy is not in fact sexual pleasure – it is not much easier under what are obviously permissive circumstances to obtain that in privacy – but not to know who is one's partner. These anonymous little figures engaged in licking, sucking, approaching each other from the rear, having intercourse standing on their heads, or with animals, give the impression of fish in an aquarium. In an orgy everyone discards their identity and plunges in a pool of dizzying anonymity. The Silpa Shastras, or scriptural manuals for the temple artificer, are so meticulous that it is hard to imagine how this meaning of the orgy scenes would have escaped them, or were tolerated merely for the sake of a bit of fun. If titillation were indeed the object of the maithunas there surely would have been nothing to stop the portrayal of orgy scenes on the same prominent and monumental scale. One can only suppose that these small orgy scenes were a deliberate counterpoint to the grand maithunas. With the development of erotic art to its fullest peak, orgiastic scenes commonly portray beautiful young women dancing and having intercourse with old men in ascetic garb. They often replace the auspicious mithunas. This has puzzled many commentators. Either it is thought that this is documentary evidence in support of erotic sculpture as inspired by sexo-yogic cults under the tutelage of a monk, or as a comment on the degenerate abuse of tantric practices. But the woman-and-ascetic is also a very ancient and exceedingly common theme of myth and literature, where sages are always encountering seductive women while practising severe austerities.

There probably is a conscious satirical element in carefully portraying the distinctive garb and hair-styles of monks belonging to well-known ascetic orders. But these sculptures seem to me to serve a similar function of counterpoint as that of the orgy scenes. In fact ascetics commonly feature in the orgy scenes. The ascetic becomes a slightly comical figure, gross, obese, lascivious, and a universal figure of fun, a *grotesque*, the very absurdity of whose pretensions as lover of beautiful young women is the antithesis of everything signified by the mutual, melting Being of the maithuna couples. Such grotesque reversals of religious ideal, added as a kind of marginalia to the affirming theme, are common the world over, and are the stock-in-trade of every band of strolling Indian players who roam the country staging plays in the villages. The bawdy humour and general jollity of both the orgy scene and the woman-and-ascetic motif are in keeping with the tendency during festivals to reverse roles. At such times priests are mocked, subservient wives bully their husbands, and the high-caste villagers are subjected to riotous indignities which at all other times would constitute a serious social offence.

6. The Cosmological Eye

The Indian temple is a wondrously complex scale-model of the Cosmos. It is always very carefully sited. Almost uncanny is the way many temples seem to have grown like plants from the soil, so welded are they to their site, so subtly positioned in the contours of the landscape. According to one ancient text 'where cows have sported with bulls, accompanied by their young ones, or where beautiful women have dallied with their lovers, that place is an appropriate site for a temple'.

For the *sthapati*, or priest-architect, building a temple is a means to bring disordered existence into conformity with the basic laws of the universe. For ourselves, a temple brings order to our individual lives and puts us in harmony with universal laws. The rules of mathematical proportion, and the layout of the images, have a rhythm and this rhythm, rather like Indian music, is conceived according to a science of moods. Even the poses of the figures carved on the temple are themselves based upon dance poses, dance rhythms, to evoke specific moods. Complex groups or clusters of images follow a rhythmic pattern across the wall surfaces like the intricate beat of Indian drums in the development of a classical *raga*. Bands of musicians are portrayed with drums, flutes and stringed instruments. Row upon row of sculpted figures sway to the rhythm of the dance, like fronds of seaweed in response to the rhythm of the waves.

The temple is an image of both the macrocosm and the microcosm – Purusha, the personified universe or cosmic man, and the purusha, or inner being of man. Temples are bodies of God; their proportions, implicit in the mathematics of the yantras, or geometrical diagrams inscribed in the foundations, are not only aesthetically pleasing but designed to relate the temples to the magical macrocosmic harmony of time and space. The various parts of the temple superstructure are designated as features of the human body: *pāda,* foot, for the base plinth; *jāṅgha* for the pilaster-like legs of the Purusha's body; *bandhāna* is a belt running round the entire structure; the *shikhara*, trunk, for the tower, with its front and back, two sides, shoulders and neck, is surmounted by a 'head' with certain distinctive features, the *amaloka*.

The devotee who visits the temple is not a tourist, an aesthete, or a gaping spectator, but a 'seer' – one who *sees*. The building blocks of the divine body are arranged in a clearly visible manner. Despite the exuberant, even florid, ornamentation, the hidden meaning of this structure is legible. Its interior can be described as a series of cavities one above the other 'like a hollow reed' or 'the cane of a hollow bamboo' as the texts put it, from the foundation to the apex. The inner trunk-cavity of the Purusha, with his viscera, especially the heart, is arranged round the vertical axis, sometimes an actual pillar, sometimes a hollow tube which is seen to emerge from the body of the temple at its apex. This detail is important, for as I said, the temple is not only an effigy of the Purusha, or personified universe, but is also an effigy of the spiritual man.

I have explained how all Indian yogic systems speak of an anatomy which is supra-physical. The yogic anatomy is the sum of experience under the special conditions wrought upon our perception through physical exercises. The *chakras* are located around the axis of the spinal column in ascending order. Cardinal to this visualized experience of the body is the hollow tube within the spinal column, felt to be a vertical channel up which courses the kuṇḍalinī, or 'serpent power'. This is the significance of the axial 'hollow reed' at the centre of the temple structure, and the successive levels of the interior cavity as well as those of the exterior (usually clusters of minor pilasters and towers intersected with horizontal niches or bands) represent the hierarchy of planes from gross to subtle, leading by degrees from the material towards the ultimate, unfathomable cause. Cosmic man and terrestrial man, macrocosm and microcosm, embrace in their being the same hierarchy of planes and values, and the temple ingeniously represents this vision of human identity with the vaster rhythms of the whole universe.

Just as the stress of the high-pointed Gothic arch induces a physical empathy of soaring spirituality, so the Indian temple can be experienced as the point of intersection between earth and sky, as both a terrestrial anchorage and an ascension heavenwards. The sculpted figures are arranged on the tower to endorse this physical sensation of the worshipper rising from earth to heaven, from darkness to light. Whether the figures are seated or standing, motionless or caught in the vortex of the sacred dance, their bodies are the visual equivalent, often literal, of yogic science. The word yoga is derived from the Sanskrit *yug*, or 'yoke'. The poses and exercises of the yogin 'yoke' him to God, bring him into union with the Absolute. In this sense all physical actions directed or 'yoked' to the divine are yogic, some literally, in the sense that they are the exercises of hatha yoga, others by analogy. Thus the movements of the dancer in the temple dance of *bhārata natyam*, or the physical positions assumed in ritual sexual intercourse, are also yoga. In the *Bhagavad Gītā* the path of good works and service to God through action is termed karma yoga.

A medieval temple has a conical tower tapering to a crest. This crest varies in emphasis considerably, but everywhere it resembles the unfolding corona of a flower's petals or the rays of the sun. This crest, or amaloka, is often one single, very intricately carved stone slab, its form explicitly derived from the lotus blossom. Architecturally, this stone serves as a formal analogy to the inner light which unfurls and 'blossoms' into an incandescent radiance at the crest of the human body – the top of the skull – when the worshipper is aroused by yogic means to a pitch of ecstasy. The amaloka is not a literal illustration of a physical event, but the nearest that the Hindu architect can visually approximate to the sensation, the 'feel', of an ineffable state quite beyond our fallible, human, descriptive powers. The experience occurs in that centre of the body situated in the skull called the *sahasrāra*, or thousand-petalled lotus. The amaloka is no more than a reminder, the barest hint, of this highest transport known to the advanced practitioner, whether yogin or mystic, in deep meditation.

The sahasrāra is flooded with bliss; so the temple tower reaches the sky as the head of the cosmic man reaches heaven. The circular stone which covers the amaloka is called the *kharpara*, the skull-bone, at the centre of which terminates the 'hollow reed' in a socket for the finial. This exactly corresponds to the *brahmarandhra*, an opening in the skull which breaks open during cremation to permit, it is said, the escape of the spirit towards final liberation after death. There are often subordinate amalokas arranged round the main tower, mostly to the number of five, comprising the five chakras through which the female serpent power ascends to unite with the male power in the thousand-petalled lotus.

The topmost finial of the tower represents the nectar which floods the sahasrāra, shining, golden, high above the garbhagṛha in an exactly perpendicular line over its centre-point. With the golden finial the limits of the world of time, of change, are reached, and with the world beyond death, the sky or heaven opens upon the Absolute, changeless region of Sat-Chit-Ānanda, Being-Conscious-ness-Bliss.

The experience of the divine light in the thousand-petalled lotus is to mystic rapture what orgasm is to sexual intercourse. Every religious tradition in India draws a clear and precise distinction between mystical ecstasy and sexual rapture, as it is commonly experienced, but a significantly large number of India's important religious sects devised methods to transmute sexual rapture into precisely, and no less than, this supreme climax of spirituality. But just as the amaloka is not a description of the thousand-petalled lotus, neither are the maithunas descriptions of sexo-yogic rites. I wish to make this point as clear as I can, because many interpreters of maithuna sculptures make the mistake of saying that the love-couples are a literal depiction of tantric sexual exercises. They are not realistic 'documentary' images of secret sex-rites. But maithunas, and likewise temple towers, and capstones, are aids or inducements to the realization of those sacred states within the worshipper.

The structure of the temple, through the cosmological eye with which it was conceived, is a formal analogy of that ecstatic rapture which is the final and most natural outcome both of yogic exercises and sexual bliss. The Hindus deserve credit for having taken the bold step of trying to *combine* these two forms of ecstasy in a third state, that of unconditioned bliss. The sculptors had recourse to a known, time-honoured language, in their case that immemorial language of magic fertility idols, to harness this basically popular folk cult for more exalted purposes than the humble artificer had ever dreamed.

Let us enter one of these temples we are considering, and approach its heart and centre. If the reader can imagine how the worshipper feels, it may then be possible to 'see' through his eyes, as Stella Kramrisch says in her book, *The Hindu Temple*, 'In its interior it has four plain walls. They are massive and their continuity is broken only by the entrances in the front wall. There is no other source of light. . . . This is the place towards which the devotee proceeds where worship is offered. This nucleus remains, poor, undisguised yet hidden, the place where dwells the Supreme Principle, as God, Iśvara, in the consecrated image or symbol.

'It is independent of time and place, a cavity held by primary elements of architecture and their relationship. . . . This secluded spot is called Garbhagṛha ("womb-house"). The name refers also to

Shivalingam, Mahābalipuram

the human body and to the inception of life. . . . The name of
Garbhagṛha is not, however, intrinsically connected with its form.
Both are symbols and each stands for an aspect of the same reality.
The use and form of the Garbhagṛha do not coincide on the plane of
things seen. They coincide in their destination. The Garbhagṛha is
not only the house of the Germ or embryo of the Temple as Purusha;
it refers to man who comes to the Centre and attains his new birth
in its darkness. The Garbhagṛha is *Rahasya*, secret and mysterious.'

    The Garbhagṛha usually contains a single image of wood, stone, or
crystal. At the very heart is an etheric space cavity, the place of
Brahman, relating also to the cavity of the heart, the centre of being
in man. In the *Chandogya Upanishad* it is said of this etheric cavity
that 'both heaven and earth are contained within it; both fire and

air, both the sun and the moon, the lightning and the stars, and whatever there is in this world, and also what is not – all that is contained within it'. 'The darkness in the Garbhagṛha is a necessary condition for the transformation which is wrought in the devotee. In darkness his change is effected and a new life is attained. . . . If then the light is waved in front of the image, this illumination is an act of recognition of the God in the potent, superluminous darkness, revealed now and known further in all the images outside on the walls of the temple, of the many gods, the Devas, the shining ones, in the light of day. The effulgence, the images of the gods, which are carved on the walls and set into their niches in the splendour of the Golden Germ, the light which shines from the Primordial Darkness.' At one Khajuraho temple a gold casket symbolized the Golden Germ. In this casket the mandala of the temple was drawn; golden fillets were used to divide its cosmic components. At its centre were placed precious stones and the attributes of the deity. Around this were four lotus blossoms, corn, pigment, and other metals. When the temple was under construction, on one 'immaculate night' the priest performed the 'rite of fertilization', and immured the Golden Germ in the wall of the Garbhagṛha.

As the temple is considered to mark the intersection of all levels of consciousness and planes – the underworld of darkness and un-consciousness, the earth and consciousness, the heavens and en-lightenment – it sometimes has a crypt or substructure beneath the Garbhagṛha, with a phallic lingam standing in water. In Orissa the name for the womb-house is *gambhira*, the deep-lying.

While this temple cosmology never departs from the 'body-language' of womb-house, cavity of the heart, spinal column, and so forth, the actual building blocks with which the structure is made consist of non-descriptive, non-realistic, geometrical shapes. The ideal beings which adorn it are modelled naturalistically on the human body. As I said before, however, they do not describe sexual techniques, ritual poses, maithuna rites. They evoke an experience which, while it has its source in the sexual act, refers to an indescribable innerness.

Only one manual for architects – these have an authority like that of minor scripture – specifically mentions the carving and siting of maithunas. It prefaces this with the doctrine that 'Desire is the root of the universe. From Desire all things are born. Primordial matters and all beings are reabsorbed [by the Creator and Destroyer of the Universe in aeonic cycles of time] through Desire. Without Shiva and Shakti creation would be a mere illusion. Without the action of Desire there would be no life, no birth and death.' The important and unusual interest of this statement is that it is explicitly associated with installation of maithuna sculptures. This reference to desire as the source of the Creation echoes those that are more ancient by at least a thousand years, long before India's sexual religiosity had developed a specifically tantric character.

We find in the *Bṛihadāranyaka Upanishad* that in 'the beginning this world was the Self alone in the form of a Person [Purusha]. Looking around He saw nothing else than himself. He first said "I am." Thence arose the name "I". . . . Verily He had no delight. He desired a second. He was indeed as large as a man and woman closely embraced. He caused that Self to fall into two pieces. Therefore this is true: "oneself is like a half fragment" as Yajñavalkya used to say. He copulated with her. Therefrom human beings were produced.'

There are several references in the Upanishads, which are among the most venerated of the Hindu scriptures, mostly composed from the seventh century B.C. over a period of several centuries, to the view that a woman should be approached as a goddess, and that sexual intercourse be performed as a sacred rite. Once again the *Bṛihadāranyaka Upanishad* is most explicit, stating the woman's 'lap is a sacrificial altar; her hairs the sacrificial grass; her skin the soma-press; the two lips of the vulva are the fire in the middle. Verily, the world of him who practises sexual intercourse knowing this, is as great as the world of him who performs the great Vajapaya sacrifice.'

A variant from the *Chandogya Upanishad* expresses the same idea in a slightly different way. 'The woman is the fire, her womb the fuel, the invitation of a man the smoke. The door is the flame, the entering the ember, pleasure the spark. In this fire the gods form the offering. From this offering springs forth the child.'

It is clear from these texts that they too have not wholly lost their link with primitive cults of fertility, but are expressed in a high-flown literary Sanskrit of the priestly caste. The *Śilpa Prakāśa* says of maithuna sculptures that 'a place without love-images [kāmakāla] is known as a "place to be shunned". In the opinion of the Kaula-caras [a tantric sect] it is always a base, forsaken place, resembling a dark abyss, which is shunned like the den of death.' It refers to a yantra, or mystic geometrical diagram, which is to be inscribed beneath the base of each maithuna couple and then sealed up. This yantra is regarded as of such potency that it will drive away 'ghosts, departed spirits, goblins, fearful demons and other hideous creatures will flee away at the mere sight of the yantra. Hear me, I am explaining this secret with great care. This yantra should never be given to anyone who is not a Kaulacara.' The author of the manual goes on to say that the yantra has to be concealed from the eyes of the profane, and for this reason the curious device was used of carving an amorous couple over it 'to give delight to people'.

A moment's reflection will show that this air of secrecy concerning the yantra, and the command to conceal it from view, is in keeping with the way sexuality is deeply associated with the deliberate transgression of a tabu. A naked communication of something so densely ringed by social convention with tabu is a notoriously dangerous business. It can, however, be quite safely attempted by employing art.

Our text refers to typical unconscious symbols – 'goblins', 'den of death', 'hideous creatures' – references to the repressed fears associated with sacrilege. Another psychological clue is that the yantra's inscription is executed in a ritual of consecration. Rites too are conventionalized acts of sacrilege. Like the hesitant lover's poem, a rite de-personalizes the private significance of an act; through artifice, dangerous and unmanageable human impulses such as sexuality and aggression are domesticated for our own development and our social survival. 'The expression of these', says Dr Alex Comfort, 'and the ability to accept them, in forms which do not make life intolerable is the chief object of all the complex emotional skills which primitive ceremony reinforces.' For example, millions of brides can accept without a blush, 'I take thee to be my lawful, wedded wife . . . with my body I thee worship', but would find intolerable 'Jane and I plan to sleep together'.

Our illustration of the yantra (see opposite) is drawn from an incised palm-leaf strip on which all Indian scriptures used to be written. The yantra looks innocuous enough, a typical example of what may correctly be called tantric art. It depicts the vertical shank of the lingam of Shiva at its centre; the triangles are yonis or bhagas, vulva or womb, designating sixteen different goddesses, whose sixteen emanations, called 'indolent nymphs', are to be portrayed in a variety of seductive poses on the exterior of the temple tower. There is an egg at the centre, in this case a device signifying the Great Goddess, Shakti. This particular yantra would be the equivalent of a seal or emblem of an esoteric sect, a sect which, because it performed the tantric maithuna rite, would constitute a sacrilegious act of transgression against the ascetic norms of orthodox Brahman Hinduism.

*Kāmakalā Yantra. Vārāhi
Temple, Caurasi, Orissa*

By medieval times maithuna sculptures would no longer carry the supercharged sacred numen of cultic idols, would not be *worshipped*. But the author of the *Śilpa Prakāśa* was a shrewd psychologist, whoever he was and at whatever date the manual was itself composed. The profusion of maithuna sculptures on temples of the period no longer constituted an emotionally loaded transgression of tabus. The yantra, on the other hand, is a different matter. Maithuna rites have always been performed in secret, and still are. The tantric sects remain on the outermost fringe of the acceptable; the very fact that their rites are a sacrilege is the source of their appeal, and without secrecy would lose their potency.

A custom of ancient Greece may shed further light on the psychology of transgression. The genuine cult idol of a Greek deity was not the artistic marble by a famous sculptor displayed to the public in the outer portion of the temple. It was a crude, inartistically hewn log, kept in a secret shrine. In the public statue beauty replaced sacredness as an alibi for the tabued material.

Art flowers in proportion to its distancing from esoteric material. Western church sculpture, for example, achieved the status and gracefulness of art when religion had distanced itself from idolatry. The most sacred image at Chartres Cathedral was an idol of the Black Virgin to which pilgrims personally offered their devotions in thousands, not to the great sculptures over the doorways, or the stained-glass windows which are the glory of the church in the artistic sense. Likewise, the yantra is a part of the cultic core of an esoteric religion, and as in the case of the crude, lumpish idols of the Hindu pilgrim shrines, its meaning is linked with the act of transgression which enhances the sacred power of the temple into which it has been embedded.

7. Indolent Nymphs

While the carved figures depict the human body, they are not images of people but of *ideal beings*. Every temple has complementary deities besides the god of the central shrine. These are to be considered to possess a special inner relationship with the main divinity. But there is a remarkable range of lesser figures and celestial damsels too: devas, danavas, pannagas, yakṣas, rāksasas, guhyas, gandharvas, vidyādharas, siddhas, kinnaras, nāgas, and apsarases. Their disposition can be as intricate as that of the figures carved over the doorways of Gothic cathedrals, and have an equally specific theme to relate. Minor divinities may form a protective ring around the temple's chief deity, are its emanations and thus illustrate its functions.

Of importance to our theme, especially on those temples influenced by tantric ideas, are the profusion of single, seductive female figures. The various sects of tantric persuasion regard the highest active principle of the universe as female, and accord supremacy to the great goddess, Devī or Shakti. That may sound a bit formidable in the context, but the fact remains that the temples at Khajuraho and many elsewhere built after A.D. 900 are profusely decorated both inside and outside with voluptuous female apsarases, celestial nymphs in indolent and provocative poses. The *Śilpa Prakāśa* enumerates sixteen types of alasākanyās, indolent nymphs, who are to be depicted with playful liveliness. Hardly what might be called the highest active principle, but at least chips off the same block of male fantasy.

At Khajuraho it is not the maithunas which set the mood but the apsarases, for while the couples turn to each other and are wholly absorbed in their love-play, the simple figures of naked women, or women in the process of stripping off their clothes, turn to face the viewer and expose their bodies, open surfaces that bloom from open

surfaces. They seem to be saying that existence is outward, giving shape to the things that lie deepest. The outside world of our bodies points the goal of outwardness. Here all India's fantasies not only of 'ideal woman' but more than that, of dynamic emergence, of birth and growth and physical grace, have been projected from, as it were, deep within the blooming flesh of the stone. The stone is carved to flower, to bear fruit, but the vehicle here is almost exclusively the human body; vegetation is portrayed in a quite offhand fashion. At Konarak, on the other hand, the erotic imagery is once again profusely interlaced with rich incrustations of floral borders, entwining creepers, and within this paradisal enclosure love ungelded by anxiety, nor put to the service of unremitting labour, emerges as a revelation, in startling contrast to the deep and dark interiority of the shrine cavity. In both cases the archetypal character of the female figures carries echoes from remotest antiquity.

In *The Hindu Temple*, Stella Kramrisch, one of the best interpreters of Indian temple cosmology, points out that 'India not only thinks in images, it builds them up in a consistent body of which the sum total is the temple. It takes them from the storehouse of memory; similar forms once used in sacred rites meet, fuse, are absorbed the one in the other and contribute their particular meaning to the new context.' She cites the adaptation of the aboriginal dolmen and the vedic altar, and how the total aspect of the building preserves 'the memory of a cult, the cult of caverns; and this corresponds moreover to the immediate realization of the cavity of the heart'.

Thus, in the case of the apsarases and indolent nymphs we have direct descendants of fertility goddesses. A common theme, the woman drawing down the branch of a tree to garland herself with, is a close relative of the ancient *śālabhoñjikā*, who by the touch of her foot brings the ashoka tree to blossom. The sālābhañjikā is the commonest, most persistent icon in Indian history, with hardly a change in three thousand years.

Alice Boner describes the nymphs as expressing 'delicate feelings of love and tenderness: one is raising her arms in nostalgia for her lover, one is standing in a door-frame and is longingly looking out for him, another feels resentful on account of his absence, one is examining her beauty in a mirror, one is inhaling the sweet smell of a lotus-flower, one is caressing a parrot or another bird. Others amuse themselves with dancing and playing instruments, still others are lost in meditation or pay devotion to a divinity. All are full of delicate charm and reflect the most intense, yet restrained emotions.'

OPPOSITE: *Khajuraho (in Indian Museum, Calcutta)*

The author of the manual which Miss Boner is here commenting on declares emphatically: 'As a house without a wife, as frolic without a woman, thus without female figures the monument will be of inferior quality and bear no fruit'.

In this sentence one detects signs of a tender human sensibility. The 'indolent nymph' is the product of a more refined sensibility than the folk cults of sex magic practised in India since time immemorial. The sculptors seem to be reaching for a much deeper understanding of both erotic sentiment and the nature and psychology of woman. To adduce how far ahead they were of their contemporaries in this respect, we should look to the villager of today, who still inhabits a world that has probably seen little change since the caste system became fully articulated in the feudal period around A.D. 500. The distinguished Austrian authority on Tantra, Swami Agehananda Bharati, was himself an itinerant monk in India in the 1950s. On foot, he traversed regions of Uttar-Pradesh, Madhya Pradesh, the Vindhyas, Hyderabad, Mysore, Bihar and Coorg – areas where important erotic sculpture is located. He describes in his autobiography, *The Ochre Robe*, how the prestige and respect universally accorded to the monk in rural India permitted him to receive confidences from women who would never dream of revealing their innermost thoughts even to their kinsfolk, still less their husbands. Complete communication on an equal basis between man and wife hardly exists in India, and what the swami has to report is not exactly encouraging: 'the romantic occidental view of the Indian male as a great lover is not borne out by the average village woman. The plaintive: "I have had seven children, I have lain with my husband for ten years, but I have not experienced at any time the bliss of which our poets speak, of which our songs sing, and against which our saints warned. I obey, because it is my duty, but I would rather be spared." In succinct Freudian terms, "I am sexually unsatisfied". . . . The village males are blissfully unaware of this complaint. There is hardly any way to communicate it to them. Although I did succeed in hinting at possible shortcomings when addressing assemblies of male villagers of the pertinent age-groups, there were blank faces on every side. The idea that a woman could be dissatisfied in spite of frequent contact and frequent offspring is unknown to the villager, nor indeed would it matter if it were known, for puritanism, if mainly theoretical, permeates the village. Conjugal sex is a duty, and if it happens to be pleasant to the male, its status is thereby lowered rather than enhanced.'

OPPOSITE: *Khajuraho (in Indian Museum, Calcutta)*

The apsaras is a perfectly crystallized collective fantasy of desirable womanhood. In vulgarized form she survives in every Indian movie, every pop religious print, every calendar – those ubiquitous mass-produced icons of the twentieth century. Permanently arrested at the age of fifteen, the apsaras is the safe, consoling, love-object and plaything of the arranged-marriage system, the child-bride. With this style of marriage as a social contract, male fantasy tends to remain permanently arrested too; schoolboy sensuality conveniently glosses over every adult responsibility, including the one and only cardinal rule of all India's venerable, much-respected and seldom heeded sex-manuals: the man must act with perfect gentleness and consideration, with but one aim, his partner's pleasure and satisfaction.

This point is stressed in the *Kāma-Sūtra*, the *Kokashastra*, and the *Anaṅgaraṅga*. The man's duty is to see that every whim of the woman is indulged. It is a matter of honour and sheer self-respect that a man should arouse a woman to the deepest ecstasy: his orgasm is merely incidental – scarcely mentioned – to the prowess with which he ensures her profoundest satisfaction. One gets the feeling in India, as one does almost anywhere in the world, that this is so often emphasized, that there exists a widespread male terror at the possibility of his failure, of his impotence, in the face of this cultural imperative, a kind of *terror sexualis*, leading, as George Moore puts it, to sad and 'furious fornications'. The apsaras, more than paired groups of lovers, goads as well as consoles: she is by nature *entirely sexual*, and thinks of nothing else but the gratification of her ceaselessly flaunted desire. Could she sing, the lavishly nubile apsaras nymphet, she would have a voice resembling that of the movie playback singer – the high-pitched saccharine tones of insistently regressive child-bride 'innocence', a lasciviousness of single-minded dedication in the role of compliant courtesan. It is remarkable, therefore, that the 'indolent nymph' is sculpted with such consummate refinement and artistry. For we know only too well that, under the hypocritical ethos of contemporary permissiveness in movies and other pop arts, the nymphet-courtesan is the epitome of the crass and vulgar sexism of India's first commercialized age. The miracle, then, is that the apsaras, as Miss Boner puts it, is still so 'full of delicate charm' and 'the most intense, yet restrained emotions'.

The social life of the medieval period was saturated with eroticism and conspicuous sensuality. Life at court in all the main medieval kingdoms of India was sumptuous and ostentatious, not least in everything connected with the festive temple arts. It was the period of gigantism in temple building, and many of these were organized

OPPOSITE: *Lingarāja Temple, Bhuvaneshwar*

as vast property-holders, with hoards of treasure and great power. Hosts of artisans engaged in ancillary industries were in the employ of the temples, let alone the very considerable numbers of priests resident at, and supported by, the big pilgrimage shrines. Both the courts and the temples employed a whole population of courtesans, temple dancers and musicians. At any one major shrine nothing less than five hundred courtesans was a common figure; some had more, and the total workforce at a temple could number 20000. Vast wealth, mostly in the form of gold and jewellery, was accumulated and is still retained; armed police guard the strongrooms, Tower-of-London style.

The institution of the temple *devadāsī*, or slave-girl of God, was a prominent feature of the life centred on the temple. These women were members of a caste – dancers, musicians, actors and sacred prostitutes – with a highly evolved tradition. Devadāsīs belonged to the temple establishment by adoption, formalized in a marriage ceremony in which they were wedded to the deity. Thereafter they acted as servants to the deity, their role being, besides assisting at the elaborate rituals, to have sexual intercourse with the Brahman priests and with pilgrims or visitors to the temple. Through this role of wife to the temple deity they were considered to partake of the sacred numen of the divinity and were the agents of transmission of the deity's sacred power to the devotee or worshipper. Just as the temple itself was a spiritual power-house, a power-dispenser for those who approached in a spirit of devotion, so the devadāsī, as wife to the temple deity, was dispensing agent of the deity's sacred power to the devotee. Whether intercourse with a sacred prostitute was undertaken for pleasure or as an act of worship, the devadāsī and the client were considered to have performed a ritual act to enhance their divine nature. The client, if a pilgrim, was a stranger and thus according to the notion that he might be God under the guise of the wanderer, he too partook of divine power.

There is a story in one of the Purāṇas of a certain king who, on meeting an ordinary prostitute (not even a devadāsī), demanded that she account for the morality of her profession. In reply she told him that it was the moral rule of her caste to perform her duty – to give pleasure conscientiously – and that this moral duty was sanctioned by God. When the king protested, she called upon God to confirm the correctness of her behaviour by making a river flow backwards, and this miraculous event duly occurred, to the startled amazement of king and courtiers.

The institution of devadāsī is also sanctioned by the Purāṇas –

OPPOSITE: *Viśyanātha Temple, Khajuraho*

sacred scriptures or compilations of myth by Brahmans, and upon the authority of which the luxurious living of the medieval temple could easily be justified. The *Bhaviṣya Purāṇa* recommends the purchase of beautiful girls for dedication to the temple. A thirteenth-century traveller, Chau Ju Kua, estimated that in the kingdom of Gujerat the number of devadāsīs singing, serving and offering flowers to the deity numbered twenty thousand.

A temple inscription in the holy city of Bhuvaneshwar states: 'by him were offered to Shiva beautiful damsels like the heavenly nymphs, in whose eyes was Kāma [god of desire], in whose mouth and waist and other parts of the body were magical powers of seduction and other charms and whose persons were decorated with ornaments'. Secular dance-dramas and classical Sanskrit plays are known from dated literary references to have been performed in the mandapa or sacred dance pavilion of temples. Dr Devangana Desai relates how ' . . . when a king wanted to enjoy a kulanari or a married woman, which he could not do without incurring social disapproval, the husband of the woman – if he did not mind – could offer the wife to the temple as a devadāsī. The king could, then, easily have her without attracting any social disapproval.'

It was the custom of the times for temple inscriptions to eulogize the sexual prowess of patron monarchs in the same bombastic terms as their martial prowess. A king of the Chandela dynasty, who built temples at Khajuraho, is praised on an inscription in a temple at Kālañjara as prodigious in his amorous activities and 'like the wind of the Himalaya mountain kisses sportively the lips of the maidens, red like the pomegranate, seizes them by their beautiful tresses, removes the garments that shine brightly on the high bosoms of the maidens, and easily dries the perspiration occasioned by sport from the brows of the fair'. 'By whom was not King Paramardī-deva esteemed? He was the god . . . like a spiritual guide in the mysteries of love. Hundreds of maidens who approached his bed, and hundreds of foes who fell at his feet, were rejected by him.'

If the fantasy of the apsaras is rooted in a tawdry wish-fulfilment of the medieval male imagination, the artistry of the sculptor is certainly graceful. One cannot help but marvel at the genial tenderness with which the artists temper their idealization of female beauty and sensual allure. This is not a unique case, of course, of masterwork emergent from a socially and psychologically ignoble context, or at least a climate perilously close to the corrupt. One has only to imagine what depths of vulgarity modern artists would resort to, given an extravagance and permissiveness comparable to that

OPPOSITE: *Viśvanātha Temple,*
Khajuraho

Viśvanātha Temple, Khajuraho

which prevailed in the Indian Middle Ages. This emphasizes that the inspiration which informs these remarkable images springs from traditions more substantial than those of profligate medieval court patronage. But when, as such motifs like the śālabhañjikā attest, we are dealing with hallowed traditions of vast antiquity which could not be trifled with, or cheapened. A heritage venerated for generations, passed from one master sculptor to another, was not likely to be seriously undermined by the passing vulgarities of royalty or aristocracy, however corrupt. In any case, this Chandela art seems to have petered out eventually, not from decadence, but under the dead hand of puritanism.

8. Khajuraho

'Khaju-rahah', meaning the 'carrier of date-palms', is the origin of the name Khajuraho, where the Chandela rulers of Bundelkhand, Kālañjara and Mahoba in central India built numerous temples between A.D. 950 and 1150. Of these, over 30 temples survive within a radius of a few miles. This magnificent assembly of temples is decorated profusely with erotic sculptures and thus comprises the most extensive of all the surviving remains of these sculptures in India. It probably never did have any rival in a quantitative sense, in spite of the fact that one could cite at least 50 places elsewhere in India, some of them already mentioned, where erotic art is to be found in profusion. Along with the great temple of the Sun at Konarak in Orissa, eastern India, the art of Khajuraho represents the finest flower of erotic Indian temples. And while we are counting this striking array of maithunas, the sheer profusion of imagery on the Khajuraho temples can be indicated from statistics compiled by General Cunningham. According to this worthy gentleman, the Kaṇḍariyā Mahādeva temple, finest of them all, dedicated to Shiva, and enshrining a marble lingam 4 feet in circumference, bears 226 statues on its interior and 646 on its exterior, most of which are around $2\frac{1}{2}$ to 3 feet in height. A high proportion of these are erotic.

The Khajuraho temples are dedicated to Shiva, Vishnu and several goddesses: there are also a group of Jaina temples, the latter being a religion founded by Mahāvīra a little before the Buddha around the sixth century B.C., with a marked ascetic bias. But this did not prevent the Jaina temples from being similarly decorated with erotic sculptures, stylistically and in concept no different from the Brahmanical temples.

The oldest temple is dedicated to the Chausat Yoginī, or 64 yoginīs, associated with the goddess Durgā and the cult of Shiva.

Yoginī-Sādhana is set out in a Tantra text. There is little doubt that Khajuraho was influenced by the Tantra doctrines, but the temples are not necessarily tantric. There are no references to Khajuraho among authoritative lists of the chief *tīrthas*, or places of tantric pilgrimage in India.

The Khajuraho temple complex is a most vivid example of temple cosmology, linked with the universally prevalent Indian idea of divine kingship, a very ancient tradition stretching back to vedic times two thousand years earlier.

The Chandela dynasty is, like so many others in India, of tribal origin. This is important, for as I indicated earlier the aristocracy is linked with aboriginal India in a cultural symbiosis, and this link is not only derived from blood kinship. The tribes of central India, notably the Raj Gonds, were highly organized, with their own powerful chieftains. They were treated with much respect by Hindu kings who probably felt they had more in common with their martial and hunting prowess than with either the sedentary feudal land-holders or the rich mercantile castes. The tribes were meat-eaters and drinkers of alcohol. In the maithuna rites of the Tantra, meat and wine were ritually imbibed. Deeper cultural links on the lines I have suggested earlier comprise the more substantial ethos which visibly informs the temple imagery.

The emergence of a feudal monarch from this twilight tribal zone was, nevertheless, hushed up in accordance with prevailing custom in Hindu society. Since the king was not only the unques-tioned head of the state, the government and the army, his territorial conquests, *digvijaya*, are cosmicized in grandiose Brahman phrase-ology. These conquests should conform to the direction of the sun's course through the four quarters of the universe; he is made a descen-dant of the sun, and accordingly eulogized as a solar monarch. Vedic sacrificial symbolism associates the king with the movement of the sun across the sky, liking the king's rule with the cycle of the seasons and his annual rebirth at the New Year rites. In the sacred texts and in the panegyrics composed by court bards, the king is described as 'father of his people' and 'husband of his realm'. Some Khajuraho sculptures show men dressed in what appears to be kingly regalia engaged in sexual play with women; this proximity to celestial figures emphasizes the sacred status of royalty. The king's amours were held to dispense divine energy amongst his subjects through sexual connection with women. In the great code of Brahmanical custom, the *Laws of Manu*, the king is described as 'a great deity in human form'; 'he must be beautiful in the eyes of his

OPPOSITE : *Devī Jagadambā Temple,*
Khajuraho

subjects as is the moon in the eyes of mankind'. His title of *rājā* is a word derived from *ranjayati* – 'he who pleases'.

An inscription at Batesvara eulogizes a Chandela chieftain, probably a tribesman by birth, in these flowery terms: 'From the eye-lotus of Atri was born the god Moon who is the ornament of the beloved husband of the daughter of the lord of the mountains. From him sprang this race which has shone with its bright fame, as if decorated with pearls. In it were born of pleasing conduct, the Chandatreya princes, who by their massive arms have crushed the hosts of enemies.' Of this chieftain it is said that the god Moon appeared to him at the age of sixteen and presented him with the philosopher's stone, which will turn iron into gold, and taught him policy. Later, legend has it, this chieftain went to Khajuraho and built 85 temples.

Five Shiva temples at Khajuraho enshrine a lingam in the main sanctuary, and from inscriptions and the number of other linga found on site, it is likely that the worship of the lingam was closely linked with the Chandela dynasty. In the Mātangeśvara temple there is a lingam 8 feet high still under worship and highly venerated during the popular annual folk festival celebrated at Khajuraho, when thousands of peasants flock to the temples from all over Madhya Pradesh.

It is a remarkable fact that the three principal kings of the Chandela dynasty associated with the building of these temples, Dhaṅga, Gaṇḍa and Vidyādhara, all lived to a ripe old age. Dhaṅga was one hundred years old, it is said, when, in accordance with a not uncommon custom, he decided to commit suicide ritually by drowning himself at the sacred confluence of the Jumna and Ganges. It is a known fact that immortality was an ideal of human beings in the Middle Ages, and there is evidence that these kings achieved longevity either by some form of sexual eugenics or by simple hormone treatment. We do not know if the kings of Khajuraho followed such a course, but there is an interesting record that King Harṣa of Kashmir received a gift of female slaves called 'goddesses' initiated into a tantric cult with whom he entertained amorous relationships, since he too was 'anxious to live for a very long time'. I was once given audience by a wizened old aristocrat and millionaire Jain lying on an immense bed like a king in his Indore palace who, my friends announced with awe, was over a hundred years old, due, they claimed, to hormone treatment. The customary male way to achieve a ripe old age (claims of up to 150 years are quite common) is said to be achieved by yoga, especially by yogic retention of semen

OPPOSITE: *Chitragupta Temple,*
           Khajuraho

in intercourse. It would seem, therefore, that we have here further evidence to support the idea that asceticism and orgiasticism are the opposite sides of the same Indian coin: *deha* – the cult of the body.

The style of architecture at Khajuraho is extremely intricate, the sculpture among the most sophisticated and refined. The temple towers are like needles shooting skywards in very elongated and slim profile. They are built with anything up to a hundred horizontal ledges, like stratified rock, to counterbalance this soaring effect.

The word 'Kaṇḍariyā' means a cave, and refers to the abode of the gods, ruled over by the Lord Shiva, on Mount Kailash in the Himalayas. An inscription concerning the donor on the Yasovarma temple dated A.D. 954 says that he 'erected this charming, splendid home of Vishnu, the enemy of the Daityas, which rivals the peaks of the mountain of snow; the golden pinnacles of which illumine the sky and on which clusters of lotuses are wafted to and fro by multitudes of banners on high poles; at the sight of which the inhabitants of heaven, met together on festivals, filled with increasing delight, are struck with wonder'. Another inscription relates how the stone image for the Laksmaṇa temple was brought all the way from the Mount Kailash region in the Himalayas with the help of Tibetan contacts.

The architectural geometry is so intricate that, in plan, the towers look like the star-forms of snow-crystals. If it is not too fanciful, I would compare them to a constellation of stars mapped out on the earth. We have seen how it is normal procedure to base the plans of temples on geometrical yantras; yantras are also used in meditation or worship as extending vertically, spatial diagrams of spiritual energy.

In the heyday of royal Khajuraho this extravagance of stonework was certainly a fitting environment in which to celebrate sumptuous festivities on the grand scale. The spacious assembly halls of the three largest temples probably served the purpose of public *rangaśālās*, where music, dance, and drama were performed on such occasions. The allegorical Sanskrit play, *Prabodhachandrodaya*, was written during Chandela rule, and was staged before King Kūrttivarman to celebrate his victory over the Chedi King Karṇa.

In this play there is a Kāpālika, a man who is a member of a tantric cult, probably of a degenerate, popularized sort such as were set up by the kings in order to cloak their royal lecheries with respectability and an aura of mystification. The play's commentary explains how these men believed that deliverance lay in unrestricted

Chitragupta Temple, Khajuraho

permissiveness, especially with women, for the Kāpālika ideal is 'to become incarnate in a form like that of Shiva and enjoy the pleasures of love with a consort as beautiful as Pārvatī [Shiva's consort]'.

The Khajuraho artists miraculously managed to maintain art's innocent eye. With sheer virtuosity they tried to excel each other in the delicate nuances of expression and minutest details of personal adornment worn by the figures. The profusion of special costumes and jewellery, the different types of poses, both seductive – in the solitary figures – and coital, the language of hand gestures, and above all the wholly distinctive varieties of expression, of glance and of movement would literally take chapters to describe. The technique, in fact, is among the most polished in all Indian sculpture. Figures,

Viśvanātha Temple, Khajuraho

both male and female, including deities, are portrayed entirely in the nude. Frontal male nudes, portrayed with sensuous refinement and attention to the details of the genitals, while rare everywhere in India, are occasionally to be found here. Clearly the climate greatly helped in the natural way in which the human body is depicted. Even when profusely jewelled, the figure retains its contours.

The work with chisel is so delicate that the sculptors, for the first time since the Gupta period, the peak of the classical age, can portray the almost impossibly fine muslins worn by wealthy women and courtesans. According to the poet Kālidāsa, the garment covering a woman's breasts was so light that it could be displaced by the breath. In his *Śakuntala* the poet describes how a woman, on seeing her lover gazing at her, put on her bodice to conceal her breasts. But her passionate feelings made it burst open, thus exposing her breasts to his great delight. In another story the women of Indraprastha were eagerly looking at Krishna arriving in the city. One of them, it is related, was standing on the roof of her house, her garment fluttering in the breeze, appearing as if she had raised a banner with her garment, in honour of Krishna. Such details were translated into stone with ease and fluency by these extraordinarily deft craftsmen. Special attention was paid to rendering skin texture in the stone, too, and a female figure on the Laksmaṇa temple bears a number of nail-marks on her breasts and armpits – nail-marks which were dwelt on so lovingly by Vātsyāyana in the *Kāma-Sūtra*.

I wrote elsewhere of Khajuraho that there is a certain aggressiveness in the waspy little nymphets; their highly stylized bodies conform to the mannered idiom of the whole, and are flexed like taut bows. The elongated slits of their half-lowered eyes give a sting to their pert and darting glances. They fling themselves on their men with the quivering metallic ardour of insects. While some embrace their partners with hesitant eagerness, thrusting their triple-curved bodies from the deep niches into the sunlight, others shyly retreat into the shadows, faces tilted with *knowing* smiles. Theirs is a less than innocent appeal to our complicity, while they watch the scenes of passionate abandonment. They are all permanently arrested at the age between girlhood and maturity.

Dr Devangana Desai is the first writer to notice how variations in the architecture are prime determinants in the selection of coital postures to be depicted: 'Thus, for example, canons of the Chandela and Orissan schools assign greater importance to the erotic motif by placing it on more visible and larger parts of the temple, while those of Gujerat confine them to unimportant places. The assignment of the motif in the temple-scheme, in turn fixes its size, which is as important a factor as the type it represents.' 'In Orissan and Khajuraho temples, erotic motifs being on the *jaṅgha* [pilaster-like, 'legs'] vary in height from two and a half to five feet, whereas in other regions they are very small, rarely more than one foot in height. . . . The artists of Khajuraho and Orissa had to be careful in the selection of poses in representing sex. The standing pose was the most suitable as it would not conflict with the rising surge of the temple. . . . The standing attitude is thus widely prevalent in representing erotic motifs on the temple. . . . It is clear that in the standing pose the lady has to be shown in front of her lover, as otherwise the larger male body would almost hide her. So when sculptors have shown the woman in the foreground in a vertical pose of union, it need not be representative of the *puruṣāyitā* [coital pose in which the woman plays the dominant role].' Given the proportions of the available spaces, sculptors were nevertheless free to indulge in all kinds of pose-representation. On the spokes of the chariot wheels at Konarak the woman takes the active role and the man lies supine, within roundels where the roles could just as well be reversed. It was possible for the sculptors to represent not necessarily how we *see* ourselves in the sexual act but how we *feel* about it. How impoverished this art would have been, says Alan Watts, had the sculptors worked within the stifling constriction of our Western 'wham-bam-thank-you-mam' style of intercourse. An interesting feature of the siting of the coital representations is the prominent repetition, one above the other, of an identical pose on two or three panels. This is in keeping with the trance-like effect of temple art, a way of conveying the pulse of rapture, its balletic or copulatory surge. A comparison here with Indian music is once again apt. Thus a *tāl* or rhythmical cycle recurs again and again. Repetition of what appear formal elements of decoration serve a highly erotic purpose.

At Khajuraho the most vigorous temples are also the most erotic, whereas in its decadence, Chandela eroticism peters out, a succinct refutation of those moralists who contend that erotic art is itself decadent.

The early phase includes the Lakṣmaṇa temple, where the maithunas are of great prominence, both on the exterior surfaces – the temple 'skin' – and in the interior, on pillars, lintels, door-jambs, cornices and gharbhagṛha wall. The upper exterior panels have depictions of a divine couple, attended by musicians. Scenes involve royal persons and female attendants who are fingering their pudenda, while ascetics dance ecstatically with comic ungainliness. There is one rare example of a recumbent pose in which the woman takes the active role, a reversal of the more common position, where she is supine and the man squats astride her. On the base there are orgiastic scenes, one of which is among the most abandoned in this kind of work. Only about one foot in height, it depicts numerous couples engaged in a wild orgy. One man who is being fellated seems to be highly pleased with himself! Three people are pounding something in a special type of vessel, possibly a concoction of bhang.

The middle phase, with the most beautiful temples, includes the Kaṇḍariyā Mahādeva, which I have already mentioned. The interior is much more complicated here. Circumambulation of temples formed an important part of all ritual worship, but the Kaṇḍariyā is a good example of the provision for an inner path of circumambulation of the garbhagṛha, for closer contact with the sanctum, and darshan of the giant lingam. Maithunas are located on the exterior wall of the Garbhagṛha. On the lower vestibule walls to the sanctum, orgiastic scenes portray couples who are helped by attendants in a gleeful state of sexual arousal. The top panels show a

Pārśvanātha Temple,
Khajuraho

man having relations with a woman, while the attendants are actively participating in the love-play. While copulating, one of the partners reaches for the genitals of an attendant, and the latter have their hands on their own genitals too.

On the southern wall of the Kaṇḍariyā we find the spectacular scene in which a man is portrayed as having intercourse which involves, it would seem, the common yogic practice of standing on the head. Dr Alex Comfort has suggested that, due to the problem of portraying recumbent poses on panels which must harmonize with the verticality of the tower, we are to envisage these couples as in fact lying down. If this is so, then the couple certainly look as if they are at their ease; but either the sculptor has 'forgotten' or has failed to portray the two attendants with legs similarly unflexed; as it is, the latter are in the usual taut posture of the standing figure. I tend to feel that this is another example of vertigo deliberately sought.

What nobody knows for sure is whether these erotic groups, with their carefully detailed portrayal of high society, are meant to be literal descriptions of royal harem scenes or refer to some religious ritual in which royalty participates – and the celestials do look more

Viśvanātha Temple,
Khajuraho

regal than divine. Almost certainly it is neither; even if some deri-
vation from real life is involved, these scenes do not depict ordinary
mortals. The presence, too, of ascetics in this group sex in no way
contradicts the idea that they are court scenes, for we have plenty of
evidence of the modern courts of petty princely states where orgies
were organized by inglorious Indian Rasputins. If the reader wishes
to imagine the psychology of the gurus, holy men, and priests who
flocked round medieval Indian monarchs, they would not be far out
if they compared these wily figures from the pages of Indian history
to the Russian monk who held the court of the last Tsar in thrall.

By this time Hindu kings must have realized that the great
military power of the Islamic peoples on their western flank was
dedicated to the destruction of idolatry. Certainly there is one
remarkable coincidence: without a doubt the two finest Indian
temples bearing erotic art are the Kaṇḍariyā and the Temple of the
Sun at Konarak. Both were constructed in a period of military
triumph over Muslim invaders. With the Chandelas it was the
defence of Kālañjara fort against Mahmoud of Ghazni in A.D. 1019
and 1022. With the Orissans it was the resounding defeat of a
Muslim army, whereby King Narasimha brought under his
suzerainty large slices of Muslim territory in Orissa and southern
Bengal.

9. Sahaja: the Rebirth of Love

The male and female figures on Indian temples symbolize nothing but themselves. They are to be taken literally, not as symbols of something else. It would be quite inappropriate for us to psychologize and say that Indians were, at that time in history, in the grip of unconscious projection, that they were 'really' trying to heal the split between warring opposites within the psyche through carved imagery that remains 'stuck' for millennia at an unconscious – i.e. 'sexual' – level. It was an entirely conscious choice to portray the sexual embrace. This choice related to practices whereby the sexual act itself became instrumental in achieving what is commonly called the 'sacred inner marriage', the *unio mystica*. There is no doubt that sexo-yogic intercourse can lead to the *unio mystica*. Something like this appears to have been attempted with increasing frequency from a period round the eighth century A.D. with the emergence of the Buddhist Sahajiyā movement. By the eleventh century this movement had spread to Hinduism; and by the thirteenth or fourteenth century it had become a major preoccupation of many religious communities in northern India, in those regions where the greatest concentrations of erotic sculpture are to be found. I would go as far as to say that this mystical trend is probably part of a much wider movement which included the Sufi aspects of Islamic religion across the entire Middle East and North African region. The *unio mystica*, or conjunction of spiritual love and the natural physical love it transmutes, is the very definition of mystic love. We shall see, in our concluding chapter, that the Temple of the Sun at Konarak bears overt signs of a major shift in the psychological climate of popular religion. Let us meanwhile examine the ideas which were to inspire this shift.

One consequence of increasing emphasis on the *unio mystica* is a decrease in the importance of ritual – very marked and intricate, for example, as ritual is in Tantra – and a greater emphasis on humanistic lyricism and tenderness in temple imagery. The erotic sensuality of Khajuraho gives way to a freer, more emotional, more *loving* model of the relationship between man and woman at Konarak.

We have referred often to *sex* but less often to *love*. There has been occasion enough to talk of eroticism, sexuality, desire, ecstasy, divine rapture. But not much has yet been said about the elusive and intangible element of love. And against all this must be set these works which, in spite of, rather than because of, a particular social climate of ambivalent sexual attitudes, remain to a surprising extent uncorrupted by morose sensuality or lewd pornography. What sustained this persistently innocent artist's eye? Art is, of course, so often an expression of our ideals rather than our attainments, so often an attempt to surmount our own failings, especially in societies where the concept of love is far from unequivocally affirmed.

The most momentous step in the evolution of Indian feeling was the Buddha's emphasis upon compassion and the sentiment of friendly concord. Next in importance, coming in the wake of the Buddha's compassionate teachings, is the concluding message of India's fervent classic of scriptural poetry, the *Bhagavad Gītā*. Towards the end of this poem is an announcement directly contrary to the prevailing ethos of that period, the third century B.C. It looks as if it has been slipped in as unobtrusively as possible. Krishna tells Arjuna: 'Listen again to My final word, the most mysterious of all. With strong desire have I desired thee; therefore shall I tell thee thy salvation. Think on Me, sacrifice to Me, pay to Me homage; so shalt thou come to Me. I promise thee truly, for *I love thee well. Give up all things of the law*, turn to Me only as thy refuge. I shall deliver thee from all evil; have no care.' The emphases are mine, and it is on these two phrases that so much in later Indian religious history which concerns us here depends. This is the earliest recorded occasion of that reckless passion which flares up in devotional and lyrical Indian poetry. However restrained his lines seem to us today, Krishna gives precedence to action prompted by the heart. The implication is that even the *Laws of Manu* are not the last word, and that caste duties, which have been both the moral muscle and the strait-jacket of human conduct in India for around two millennia, give way before oracular revelation, the word of God, the still small voice uttered deep within the heart.

The consequences of the teachings of Buddha and the *Gītā* were incalculable. We have seen how Buddhism tenderized the fertility cults. The *Gītā* set in motion a wave of devotional fervour – *bhakti* it is

OPPOSITE: *Chitragupta Temple,*
Khajuraho

called – which runs like a second river alongside the far sterner, even intricate and endlessly supple current of Brahman and monkish orthodoxy – the Jumna and Ganges respectively of formal Indian religion, the Jumna flowing in a far easier, informal way, meandering around, but at times in open defiance of the formidable caste regime, flooding over its banks in the Middle Ages. It is not the way of India to mount direct confrontation with orthodoxy, even though heretical sects proliferate. Religious history on the sub-continent is a swirling, converging, fusing and redividing amalgam of orthodox, heterodox and heretical sects. Brahmanism and bhakti always run the risk of petrifying in defensive postures and of losing their living fluidity, just as did the Church and the heresies in European history. It is the molten power of human emotion which erupts from the unconscious, or from the subterranean social strata, the disinherited on the borders of society, even tribal elements of the culture. This fecund subsoil culture of the folk, which I call the social antipodes, provides the Indian peoples, so prone to codification, pedantry, formalism and rigidity, with gentler feelings.

The broad base of Indian culture always has been – and still is – rural and agricultural. The cities, the courts, the feudal dynasties provide the sophistication which we have seen in the refinement and artistry of the temples. But at heart India is both idolatrous and passionate, in the grip of the emotions more than of the reasoning or intellective faculties. The Brahmans were codifiers and synthesizers. From vedic times onward, the creative thrust came from lower on the social scale. And because at all times the population of peasants has never been less than the overwhelming majority, religion obstinately retains traits of the peasant mind, peasant preoccupations, semi-primitive, never completely de-tribalized, and all under the sign of Eros. Sex is the most direct, the most volcanic, vehicle for pent-up feelings. Every feature of the mass culture is saturated with sexuality.

But even here, in the underground culture, we see a dialectic between the mythological imagination with its persistent cathexis on the cultic idol, and the lyrical fluidity of feeling – bhakti – the sacred vortex of emotion which sweeps all before it, overturns the idols and, as in the poems of the Ālvārs in South India, soars into mystical rapture which, to quote Zaehner, 'in its frank sexuality, is really comparable to that of the great Christian mystics like St Teresa and St John of the Cross in a way that the introspective mysticism of the *Yoga-Sūtras* and the Vedānta is not'.

The main period we are dealing with, feudal India, saw the emergence in connection with that grand opera of the sacred arts, the

medieval temple, several distinct and powerful religious movements
from deep sources in the antipodes. These come under the heading
very broadly speaking, of either Tantra or Sahajiyā. Both bear
aboriginal traces, both are fired by the emotion of bhakti, and both
share a single common practice: yoga. It is yoga, both in a psychological and a practical, even physical sense, that sustains them more
than ritual.

Now yoga is a cult of *power*, in this case a power of fusion, an
attempt to fuse together mind and body. It can be used equally well
to develop sexuality as to suppress it, to enhance it so that it becomes
indistinguishable from mystical ecstasy – *is* mystical ecstasy – or to
overtake it and enter a very strange state, a kind of supra-sexual
rapture which has about it an unearthly glow, a quality which
pervades the best temple sculpture too, and persuades us that there
must be a love which is a secret between God and the soul that has
never been wholly divulged, whether in words or in images. Now and
then, when the sun caresses the flowering limbs of temple walls, my
eyes follow the glances in the lovers' eyes and I can glimpse the
light of that wordless love which is a refracted spark of their delight-
drunken rapture.

The main point about the Tantra and Sahajiyā movements is that
they are *esoteric*. They are ringed with secrecy to protect something
very delicate, very intimate, that can only be transmitted from
person to person. In that twilight zone, communication is accom-
plished by gesture, tone of voice, silence, vibration of vocal sound
through mantra – a kind of sonic spell – and personal charisma – a
current of mingled love between members of a warmly close circle.

The process is of a piece with the doctrine; here again, the basis
of the doctrine is the same, no matter what the school or sect: the
absolute reality possesses a dual nature, the static and the dynamic,
rest and activity, the enjoyer and the enjoyed, seed and ovum. In
pure Being these two aspects lie unified together, but at the level of
time and change – ordinary existence – they are separate, in a state
of bondage, of suffering, of anguish. The course of action is to achieve
liberation from these contrary stresses and attain the final state of
non-duality. The secrecy and the closed circle are stringently
imposed, since it is in dialogue, in intimate partnership, that *people*
experience this fusion in communion together. In orthodoxy,
worship is solitary. In the esoteric schools the basic unit is the pair,
or a circle of pairs – the guru and the disciple, the guru and the
circle, or pairs of disciples with the guru, or pairs alone. Herein lies
the danger, the source of friction with society at large, and the fuel

for the flames of what often developed into the attainment of incandescent powers. We come close to this quality of intense group communion today in what we in the West call the Encounter Group. Anyone who has experience of such group work will understand both why a group is a closed circle, and why it inevitably exists in tension with society at large.

Solitude is the irreducible fact of the human condition. Man knows he is alone, but longs to realize himself in another. He searches for communion. In India the great problem is how to do this within a caste-bound society, and the solutions are obvious. One who seeks communion at the deepest level can only do it either by finding a guru or a partner of the opposite sex. The potency of the Indian esoteric schools lies in the fact that they seek to obtain *both*. Through the esoteric circle the communicants re-establish the bonds that united them with life in a past and future paradise. Here we can clearly see that temple imagery almost literally fleshes out this yearning, is expressed in the vocabulary of love. It is love which, pre-eminently, grants us an instant of true, of full life, in which all anguished contraries and separateness dissolve.

In India, as much as anywhere else, if not more so, love is an almost inaccessible experience. The caste system, ethnic and sectarian differences, occupation and role, everything implied by Krishna's 'all things of the law', conspires against love. Even the relations between the sexes are vitiated by contrary stresses. No country in the world surpasses India in its tendency to idolize its projections of its own confusions on the opposite sex, to construct gods and goddesses out of these fantasies which veil the true nature of the other, the 'be-loved'. The enjoyer casts a blight upon the enjoyed of inextricably confused false perception. The woman, in particular, is recipient of a barrage of fantasy that does not correspond to her reality as a person and forces her to retreat into docile servitude. She can only occupy the role man has invented for her. So constituted, it is small wonder that it is the rules of this 'society' which love itself must transgress.

The Indian marriage is a social contract arranged by the society and thus inimical to love. I have seen bride and bridegroom sit, a neglected pair, in the Hindu temple, while the elders and their lawyers sit over the account books, to bargain for a satisfactory deal between the two families, and to dole out banknotes from portable metal safes.

The esoteric circles held a centuries-long debate over the respective merits of conjugal relationship between man and wife versus ritual relationship between partners whose marriage partners were either

Sūrya Temple, Konarak

elsewhere in the circle or not included. In all such circles, the extra-marital bond won. This too is yet another factor in the necessity for stringent secrecy.

Through sheer durability and proven efficacy as a system of regulation, the caste denies the profoundest instincts of its members. True, it professes to serve their needs, but history has shown, not through revolutions but through explosions of religious fervour, that whole classes, communities, minorities have done more than just chafe under its regime. One has only to observe any ordinary social gethering, in any class or caste, in city, town, or village, to appreciate to what devastating extent social life prevents almost every possibility of achieving relationship of mutual and equal regard.

Countless sturdy independent spirits must have looked around them at the pattern of introspection and solitary devotion with which the religious scene in India presents them at every turn, and realized that it possessed about it a narcissistic insensitivity to sharing and deep togetherness. The instinctive response was, of course, to start again from scratch, to concentrate upon the microcosmic quality of relations between man and woman.

There were plenty of individuals who undertook their own personal quest to restore the lost sense of unity by applying their yogic experiments consistently and in an inclusive sense. For all its heavy-handed sensuality, and its male glorification of female power, Tantra is a psychologically motivated attempt to regain some kind of balance between male and female principles.

But the more widespread, emotionally fervent Sahajiyā movement went much further than Tantra to harmonize the male and the female principles not only in marriage but in every conceivable aspect of everyday life, and in all social interaction. Like Tantra, the Sahajiyās were both Buddhist and Hindu. It is the latter that we will find so illuminating to the whole theme of love between man and woman. Here, it is worshippers of Vishnu in his most genial incarnation, Krishna, who make the major contribution of the Middle Ages to the development of a mystical love cult which is at the same time humanistic. Its origins can be traced back to the *Bhagavad Gītā* of the third century B.C., but the Sahajiyās emerge late, at the same time as erotic sculpture attained its apogee.

The Sahajiyās give expression to a form of love which goes by the name of *sahaja*. This may be translated as 'togetherness', 'spontaneity', or 'effortless being'. It implies everything that is relaxed and natural, straightforward or direct. In this system the natural qualities of the senses should be utilized. The dual principle of male and female is personified not in Shiva and Shakti but in Krishna and Rādhā. In his *Obscure Religious Cults*, a leading authority, S. B. Das Gupta, tells us how the Sahajiyās hold that all men and women are physical manifestations of Krishna and Rādhā, and that this 'realization of the true nature of man as Krishna and that of woman as Rādhā is technically known as the principle of *āropa* or the attribution of divinity to man. Through continual psychological discipline man and woman must first of all completely forget their lower animal selves and attribute Krishnahood to man and Rādhā-hood to woman. Through this process of attribution there will gradually dawn the realization of the true nature of the two as Krishna and Rādhā. When man and woman can thus realize themselves as Krishna and Rādhā in their true nature, the love that exists between them transcends the category of gross sensuality – it becomes love divine, and the realization of such an emotion of love is realization of the Sahaja.'

The typical Indian emphasis on the body is still very much to the fore. The attainment of sahaja presupposes the strength and special vitality of the body achieved through stringent, rigorous and lengthy yogic training. Pure love, along with a perfectly tuned body, is the best and highest method through which direct communion with God becomes possible. This love for God, love absolutely for love's sake, naturally minimizes the formalities, ceremonial and social conventions in religion. The great Bengali poet of sahaja, Chandīdas, proclaims this humanism in rousing terms: 'Listen O brother man, there is no truth higher than man!' Rādhā and Krishna are not considered as deities to be worshipped – 'they represent principles to be realized in humanity' (S. B. Das Gupta).

The devotee identifies with the *gopīs*, the cowherd girls who love Krishna, or with Krishna's favourite among the gopīs, Rādhā. Like the gopī, the worshipper longs with ardent passion for union with his – or her – beloved Krishna. In spite of their love for Krishna, the gopīs are married women. Transgression always heightens religious fervour. In the Krishna cults this transgression not only has its source in sexuality, but in the ideal of parakīyā love. This is, in the words of Das Gupta, 'the love that exists most privately between couples, who are absolutely free in their love from any consideration of loss and gain, who defy the society and transgress the law and make love the be-all and end-all of life'. Parakīyā love is the highest and most intense form of love; according to the sahajin it is incomparably more exalted than the love attainable within the Hindu marriage system. For this reason it is no longer tolerated by civil law, but is quite widely practised in secret.

Identification of the male worshipper with the gopī implies the assumption of the female role, not only as in Christian mysticism, with its yearning of the soul as the bride of Christ, but also that the sexual roles are reversed in the sahajin relationship of man and woman. There is a highly pertinent myth which figures in the *Bhāgavata Purāna*: in one of the deity Vishnu's incarnations he changes sex, taking the form of the divinely beautiful woman Mohinī, 'the bewilderer of the senses', in order to seduce certain demons who claimed the ambrosia that gives the gods immortality. Mohinī also seduced Shiva, Lord of Ascetics, chief deity of orthodox Brahmanism. The story is revealing, because it gives expression to the psychological

Sūrya Temple, Konarak

need to integrate into our conscious selves those unacknowledged elements of the opposite sex. It also implies the way, through the female aspects of ourselves, we must soften the excesses of the demonic and importuning will. It is typical of Vishnavite religion – Krishna being another of this deity's incarnations – that the phallicism, arrogance and domineering features of male psychology are considerably less in evidence.

The Sahajiyās make it a condition of the order 'that a man must do completely away with his nature as a man and transform his nature to that of a woman before he takes the vow of love'. The discipline of the Sahajiyā worshipper includes serving the woman as Rādhā, both literally and in the ways in which a worshipper serves a deity. But the relationship of man and woman is the starting point for a complete re-ordering of perception and conduct in every sphere of life. The true devotee of Krishna is merciful and harms no one; he is 'as humble as grass; he is truthful; he is charitable, gentle, holy, a friend and benefactor to all, moderate in all things, poetic, skilful, and silent'. This re-education of the feelings did not lead to the carving of temple sculptures which explicitly portray the sexo-yogic union of the Sahajiyā worshippers, any more than did Tantra. Yet there is no doubt that the influence of the movement on erotic art was extensive. This was notably the case among the orders of people who took holy vows, the devotional poets and wandering minstrels, and the bands of craftsmen who attached themselves to the courts and the temple institutions. The repressed lyricism of caste India was given fresh voice by a movement that was avowedly anti-caste.

Especially important in this movement was the idea that the emotion aroused by sacred art could lead the worshipper to a higher level of awareness, even to the attainment of liberation through contemplative rapture provoked by the sacred icon. One version of the story of the origin of the Ganges recounts how Shiva was aroused to such a pitch of bliss on hearing the divinely melodious music of Vishnu that he dissolved in water, and from this sprang the goddess Ganga. Art is regarded as a material aid towards enlightenment, and one who attains such a state of contemplative tranquillity is known as 'the motionless one'.

10. The Temple of the Ray-Garlanded God

On the sixth day of the bright fortnight of the lunar month of Magh, in January or February, thousands of rural folk set off in their bullock carts along the old Orissan shore route to the temple of the Sun, at Konarak. The journey through the night takes them many hours, the bells on their huge hump-backed beasts jingling in the cool moonlight, the wheels creaking with that ancient sound one comes to associate with this immemorial sight of pilgrims on the move. The wheels of their carts have furrowed tracks across India which are still in use thousands of years later, even when modern highways offer more comfortable routes, simply because that has always been the way it was done. It is considered a positive virtue to follow in the grooves of another man's tracks down sacred paths of immeasurable antiquity.

These pilgrims have come to worship at a spot sanctified by the sun god since prehistoric times and known as Arka-Kshetra or Konarka, Arka being one of the many names of Sūrya, the great vedic deity of the sun. It is the time of the spring festival to celebrate the new birth of Sūrya. The pilgrims will take a holy dip in a shallow pool, or possibly in the sea, only a couple of miles away from the temple across rolling sand-dunes. Then they will approach the immense and crumbling hulk of the Sun Temple, watch the sun rise over the sea eastwards, and worship the primeval images of the nine planets.

On this day, says a legend, Samba, son of Krishna, having been cured of leprosy through the purifying grace of the sun god, offered grateful worship on the bank of the local Chandrabhaga river, now dried up. Once a prosperous seaport, Konarak has associations deeply interlaced with the folk cults of the Oriya people. The culmination of Kalinga architecture, the Temple of Sun, was built by King Narasimha Deva, who reigned from A.D. 1238 to 1264. A temple chronicle calls it 'the temple of the ray-garlanded god'.

There is some speculation that Narasimha Deva may himself have been cured of leprosy, and that there is some personal link of this kind between himself and the auspicious Arka-Kshetra. There is no doubt, however, that this grandest expression in stone of an entire Indian people was conceived in a mood of triumphant celebration, after their king had resoundingly defeated their Muslim enemies and wrested back from the foreigners their own ancestral territory. While in its religious symbolism the Konarak temple is conceived as the victory of the sun over the dark forces of evil, its imagery also is symbolic of a royal military victory. In minor key it portrays on small panels an abundance of war-scenes, armies, cavalry, elephants, armed infantry, and war-horses crushing enemies under their feet. Amongst its many marvels, it possesses some of the finest free-standing monumental life-size sculptures of horses and elephants in all Indian art. But the temple primarily symbolizes the universally fructifying and creative power of the sun. It is therefore beautifully appropriate that it has the most prolific erotic representation of any medieval temple. It is a veritable poem on that dialectic of man's most powerful emotions, sexuality and aggression, and of the seasons of war and peace.

There is a very widespread custom in India of constructing wooden festival chariots, most intricately carved with deities, including their immense wheels. Orissa is, of course, particularly renowned for these chariots, for the great annual procession of the Jagannath festival at Puri has given our language the word *juggernaut*, to describe any powerful on-rolling force or war-machine which crushes all before it. The wooden temple chariot has, in fact, no martial associations, but is an effigy of the chariot of the gods.

The Konarak temple, uniquely, is constructed of stone to resemble a juggernaut, a gigantic solar chariot with twelve pairs of wheels drawn by seven spirited horses. We are to imagine it, in the words of the poet Mayura, as

> The chariot of Sūrya ascending the pathway of the sky
> in the morning, drawn upwards by his horses.

A notable feature of the temple is the wide syncretic origins of its symbolism in the deepest soil of the popular imagination. This is a peculiarly Orissan phenomenon. Orissa is probably the least spoilt region in India; its remote rural regions, tribal and semi-tribal, are rarely visited, but preserve the atmosphere of ages past in a rustic environment of utmost simplicity, where tribal exuberance is still a living, felt force. The cult of the sun god, as the personalized form

OPPOSITE : *Detail with chariot wheel. Sūrya Temple, Konarak* of the Dharma, or Universal Law, is still widely prevalent in Orissa, linking the folk to a stratum of culture which reaches back to the time of the Buddha, who was popularly regarded as the living incarnation of Dharma, his teaching the 'spinning of the Wheel of the Law'.

The year when I first 'discovered' Indian art and culture, unaware of the Orissan cult of Dharma, I painted a Wheel of the Law, the mandala form of which was derived from the great chariot wheels of the Sun Chariot at Konarak. Was I perhaps dreaming my way unconsciously towards the deeper symbolic vision which pervades this temple? For me, as for many others in the West, Konarak is the sculptural apotheosis of everything held dear in Indian culture.

Narasimha Deva's successful fight with the Muslims must have stimulated him to construct a building unprecedented for its audacity. The story goes that it took the revenues of twelve years to finance; it certainly took sixteen to build, and its tower was seventy-five feet high. A green chlorite slab, on which were carved the emblems of the days of the week, with the ascending and descending nodes, was excavated in the hills, and had to be carried, Stonehenge-style, eighty miles across swamps and unbridged rivers. A technical innovation was the use of iron rods to fortify the masonry of the pyramid-shaped roof. A number of massive iron beams were found on site, one being thirty-five feet long and weighing ninety tons! 'The builders had a clear appreciation of the advantages of iron and knew how to apply it to good effect. . . . The realization of such a vast temple was, however, beyond the technical possibilities of that era. Even before the tower was completed the foundations subsided into the soft sand of the dunes. The shikhara [tower] collapsed. . . .'

Superb! What more fitting climax to a venture which, from the very beginning, had been a reckless affirmation of that strength which must continually be spending and endangering itself. Nothing like it was ever attempted again. Konarak is the finest of all Indian monuments informed by the eye of love. If the climax was partly tragic, perhaps it was also a perfectly appropriate fate. The temptation was irresistible: to achieve an impossible balance between the deepest sexuality and the highest eroticism, within an ordered building mirroring an ideal of an ordered society. But temptation is the desire to fall, to expend energy to the very limits, until there is no firm foundation left.

One senses that the architects knew perfectly well how impossible their plan was. At Khajuraho the towers are set on very high and massive bases. In consequence the infinitely desirable creatures which beckon and allure the eye of the pilgrim are distanced, high up, inaccessible. Their smiles even have a supercilious air. But at Konarak, a vision of the folk, the figures are not *above* the base, they are *on* it, often within reach of the worshippers' hands. Gone are the supercilious airs and graces; the couples are so very human, faintly humorous, even awkward and . . . yes . . . *shy*. How could the masons possibly, on their comparatively delicate, almost hastily extemporized platform, provide the sheer mass of awesome masonry adequate for so stupendous a tower's ascent? As it is, we have them still, and only at arm's length, these gravely playful couples, at the cost of a giant stone pinnacle.

James Ferguson, who visited Konarak in 1837, when a portion of the great tower was still standing, but had gone by 1869, wrote: 'The play of light and shade for its bold and varied projections and intervening shadows give it a brilliant and sparkling effect.' The celebrated poet, Rabindranath Tagore, writing of his visit, said: 'I step inside the sanctum, there is not one picture inscribed there, nor any kind of light, the image of the god is shining there, in the midst of silent unadorned obscurity.' The granular stone, pitted by erosion year by year, as seen in the evening light, suggested to another member of the remarkable Tagore family that it was 'built with the gold particles of the sun'. In a recent book by Miss Boner and Dr Sharma Das, *New Light on the Sun Temple*, they consider that Konarak 'expresses all shades of feeling, from adoration of the transmundane and divine to admiration of royal glamour and splendour, from exaltation of living beauty to the passions and emotions of ordinary worldly life. Even the queer, the odd and the grotesque, treated with a superior sense of humour, are not out of bounds. In the acceptance of life in all its aspects the imagery has . . . adopted the view of Sūrya himself to whom nothing is hidden, who looks upon everything in perfect equanimity, who smiles upon life and recognizes the inevitable necessity of opposites in the interplay of light and darkness. . . .'

Who, then, is Sūrya, rather remotely shining down the shaft of time upon us from India's ancient past? There is a very imposing standing image of Sūrya at Konarak, carved in polished green chlorite of a hard density quite distinct from all other statues on the structure. But the sun god has an air of obsolescence amidst the glowing humanism. Fine carving as it is, the style is rigidly stiff and formalized, almost glacial. This is an icon with the quality of a cultic image, stern, unapproachable, austere – to be appeased rather than adored. Sūrya presides impassively over the dawn of a fresh, youthful spirit. The new humanistic trend, on the other hand, emerges into the common stream of Indian culture from deep in the social antipodes. This would soon find expression mostly in poetry, literature, and miniature paintings, save for this first, sole, glorious exception in the temple at Konarak. Sūrya harks back to the Vedas at least two thousand years earlier; the Konarak lovers gather into themselves the sun god's vital energy – a transmutation of power into love – showing the way ahead. Each stage in the story of Sūrya's transformation over the millennia reveals a major shift in the psychological climate of successive historical phases.

The story begins in the *Ṛg Veda* with a verse known as the Gayatri Mantra, which every Brahman must recite each morning at the commencement of his prayers, facing the rising sun. Translated into 'poetic' English it is usually rendered thus:

Let us adore the light of the Divine Sun. May it enlighten our minds.

But it also has the meaning of: 'O Truth with the visage of the Gold Disc, remove the mist of ignorance that I may see you face to face.'

The sun god occupies an exalted position in the Vedas, and has many names besides Sūrya and Arka. As Savitri, 'he opens existence, life succeeding life'. 'He has stretched out his arms to all folk on earth.' As Pūṣan, he is sustainer and nourisher of all life, the divine herdsman, who leads his cows to opulent pastures. In a later vedic hymn:

> Sūrya hath harnessed to his car to draw him seven stately
>   bay steeds gay with golden housings,
> The Bright One started from the distant region, dispelling
>   gloom, the God hath climbed to heavens . . .
> The constellations pass away like thieves in the night
>   before the all-beholding Sun . . .
> Soaring and speeding on his way, refulgent, unwasting light . . .

By the time of the Upanishads a millennium later, the cosmic vision of the Vedas deepens into philosophical speculation about the universe, and man's inner relation to its essence. 'There are two forms of Brahman,' we are told in the *Maitri Upanishad*, 'Time and Non-Time. What was before the Sun, that was Non-Time, destitute of parts. What is preceded by the Sun, that is Time, possessing parts. The form of that which possesses parts, that is the Year. . . . This embodied Time is the Ocean of creatures. Yonder Lord, called the Sun, abides therein as its cause, from which are born the Moon, the planets, the year and the rest. . . . Whatever is seen in this world of good or evil comes from these. Therefore the soul of the Sun is

OPPOSITE: *Sūrya Temple
Konarak,*

Brahman. Therefore let a man worship the Sun under his name Time.'

The Sun is also described as both a cosmic and a human spiritual energy in the same Upanishad. 'Prajāpati bears himself two-fold, as the Spirit here, and yonder as the Supernal Sun, Yonder Supernal Sun is verily the outer self, the Spirit is the inner self. Hence the motion of the inner self is to be measured by the outer self . . . and conversely the motion of the outer self is to be measured by that of the inner self. For thus it has been said: that Golden person who is within the Supernal Sun and who from his golden station looks down upon the earth is even he who dwells, consuming food, in the lotus of the heart.'

This recalls the idea of the Golden Germ, primordial luminosity of the deity in the darkness of the temple womb-house, and of each worshipper 'yoked' to the body of the temple, as the temple is 'yoked' to the divine.

Thousands of years later, again, around the time the temple of the sun god was built at Konarak, the sun cult had given place to an introspective concern with the light of the inner self, both in the Tantra and Sahajiyā movements. Boner and Das have translated into English some lines of verse from the unpublished *Sūrya Tantra:*

> Sūrya is the very Self of the Self, travelling in the
> chariot of living beings.
> The wheel is the very Self of Time, the seven horses
> are the Life-impulses of creatures.
> Consciousness, Energy, Karma, Activity, Intellect,
> Strength, Discrimination.
> The All-pervader, seated on a luminous seat, travels
> across the whole world. . . .

The wheel of the sun chariot is called the Sādhanā-Wheel in this text. The yearly progress of the sun on the path of the constellations is compared with man's progress along the stages of yoga. 'Aries corresponds to the stage of bhakti, Taurus to the essence of delight, Gemini is Love, Cancer the Withdrawal from worldly attachment, Leo the achievement of Mastery, Virgo is mental introspection, Libra is Evenmindedness, Scorpio is Firmness of Conviction, Sagittarius is one-pointed Concentration, Capricorn deep Meditation, Aquarius the Extinction of thought, Pisces the Realization of Suchness, the Merging into the Supreme Being.'

The inner yoga path follows its course upwards through the chakras – psychic centres of the body – the inner sūrya modified at each stage in the ascent and named according to the various qualities

OPPOSITE: *Sūrya Temple,*
Konarak

of the centres, with the climax reached in deep ecstasy at the top of the cranium, where Sūrya is called Mahāvishnu-Bhāskara. 'Thus,' says this tantric text, 'Sūrya is "Lord of the Sūryas" – this Bhāskara whose body is like burning fire, seated on a lotus throne studded with gems, wearing a bejewelled crown.' An image of Mahābhāskara was, in fact, enthroned in the shrine of the small Padmakeśara temple, adjacent to the main shrine at Konarak.

The idea of the inner sun, the Mahābhāskara, related to the supernal sun, was ingeniously translated into Konarak's stone imagery. While the whole temple is an effigy of a chariot, it is a kind of cosmic calendar too, its parts composed of different measures of time, from seconds to aeons. The tower rests on twenty-four wheels, but is itself a giant wheel which we are to imagine from above, in the way enjoined on the worshipper with all such structures, as a solidified radial *mandala*, its spokes like the rays of the sun's vital energy. The sun god, being connected by aerial cords to Dhruva, the pole-star, revolves around the earth like a potter's wheel. Every detail corresponds with Hindu astronomy and cosmology. The twelve pairs of wheels, for example, stand for the twelve dark and twelve bright halves of the Indian lunar calendar.

Sūrya, as portrayed in the stern green chlorite image, polished to such a high gloss that it shines, is to be viewed as having invisible feet, covered by their own effulgence. The convention for this is a kind of boot-like sheath. The *Sūrya Tantra* indicates how the sun god is to be worshipped, each portion of the deity's body being an ascent towards the peak of ecstatic experience, starting from the formless, orange-coloured, lower world, passing through the molten gold of the self-unfolding universe in the torso, to a flash of lightning at the uppermost celestial region in the god's head.

The exterior surfaces of the temple are peopled, like the chariot of the gods, by celestial couples and dancing nymphs in accordance with popular mythology. There is, for example, a legend of the sage Kardama who had ignored his wife, the amorous Devahuti, since he had taken a vow of chastity. In response to her wishes for intercourse, Kardama projected into the heavens by magical yogic powers a celestial chariot filled with beautiful girls. He lifted his wife into the chariot, divided himself into a host of proficient lovers, and passed many years in amorous dalliance with both his wife and all the other women. The issue of this celestial interlude was Devahuti's son, Kapila, founder of the Sāṃkhya system of philosophy which served as the intellectual basis for subsequent Brahmanical aspects of the Tantra cults. This tale is contemporaneous with the building of Konarak. Typically, it recognizes the differences in the public's capacity to understand symbolism. There is a choice between a popular legend, with voluptuous attention-getting details like buxom maidens, and intellectual point-scoring for clever Brahmans in the cunning lineage it invents: respectable, 'ascetic' Kardama begets what conservatives might otherwise condemn as 'dangerous' tantric cults, thus getting the best of all possible worlds without blatant contradictions.

But when we pass from this rather crude tale of ascetics and voluptuous passengers on the celestial omnibus to the lovers depicted on the Konarak chariot, we find the greatest subtlety. The statues are far more sexually explicit than any textual account of a myth, and yet so much more delicate. The difference is that the sculptors were artists, not Brahmans. The temple represents every possible variety of sexual congress in India's considerable repertoire, including frontal positions, standing, sitting and, notably, in the wheel spokes of the chariot, recumbent too. There is a frequency of images showing oral sex – fellatio, cunnilingus and mutual mouth congress – but with a delicacy superior to that of any other temple representation of these acts. Our illustration (p. 149) is a fine example. How delicately does the calm-faced man bend a little at the knees, his arms like the branches of a shady tree, one hand – a dancer's hand – in a gesture of delighted appreciation, the other affectionately stroking the woman's hair. And she – look how she nestles comfortably, her hand placed so sensuously on his foot, the other barely touching his hand as she reaches round his thigh. A suggestion of indrawn breath, at the moment of motionless balance in a *pas-de-deux*, converts what could have been a summary description into a scene of real human warmth.

The loving couples clustered like stalactites round the base of the temple seem to turn their faces towards each other in a rapture of delight, as if each were to the other the very face of the sun, whose worshippers they all are. Their placid, round, Oriya features are discs of gently smiling warmth. In their balletic dance of love they enact the delicious movements of night's deep secret, but do so in the blazing light of the Maker of Day. This luminous rite has a thoroughly human simplicity, and for this reason the word 'ecstasy' is not wholly appropriate. There is no 'fun' in ecstasy – a state, moreover, that usually attains its peak in solitude, whereas here we have a veritable throng of lovers.

A marvellous touch is the profusion of impossible beings mingling with the human couples: chimaeras, fairies, sprites, gryphons,

monsters. They are engaged in a game of reflections to and fro between the corporeality of human lovers and dreams of incorporeal denizens of a Beyond. The lovers' closely embracing limbs seem to be melting into this extra dimension the other side of time.

A prominent feature of Konarak eroticism is to be found in maithunas of *nāga* snake deities, interlaced round pillars in representations of extraordinary sweetness. The nāga has a human head and torso, with a long serpentine body and tail. From time immemorial the nāga has been an extremely popular theme with temple artists. They are very often sculpted with a particularly loving touch, excelling the quality of other images in the shrines which they embellish.

Curt Maury has pointed out that the *nāginī*, dynamic female of the species, is to Indian eyes the epitome of female eroticism and sexuality. He shows how the nāginī is identified with the principle of infinite and continual transformation, and that it is less the aboriginal fertility or reproductive significance of the nāginī which is so lavishly celebrated, than the erotic aspect of her nature. The 'enchantment transfigures the Indian temple with an intangible accent of inward ecstasy and supernatural sensuousness. Placid with otherworldly beatitude, or again vivid with the consciousness of feminine allure, the nāginī likeness conjures an aura of extrasensory exaltation that seems to encompass the sacred precinct like the disembodied yet inextricable coils of an immense serpent. Enthralled before its presence, strangely stirred, even the casual pilgrim seems to tarry. Nowhere is this spell quite as compelling as in the sanctuaries of Bhuvaneshwar and Konarak. Here the vision of the nāginī has achieved its surpassing materialization . . . nowhere has the dynamism of the feminine essence been rendered so explicitly or so uncompromisingly.'

Nobody can remain immune or indifferent to this celebration of shared intimacies and breathtaking nakedness. The viewers' involvement is assured by the quality of effect which sexual depiction, so manifestly unexploitative, yet so blithely open, arouses. We identify willy-nilly with these antics – our laughter is quite unhostile – a response no doubt derived from our own memories of physical love. These remembered moments are intensified by art, raised to a pitch altogether more pristine than our fumbling in the carnal vortex. Warmed as we ourselves are, as we walk round the ruins, by the self-same sun irradiated from their sweet faces, so too, through our empathy with the act of love, do they become mirrors of the sun's divine luminosity. Like Rilke's angels, they are:

OPPOSITE: *Nāga couple, Sūrya*
Temple, Konarak

Early successes, favourites of fond Creation,
ranges, summits, dawn-red ridges
of all beginning, – pollen of blossoming godhead,
hinges of light, corridors, stairways, thrones,
spaces of being, shields of felicity, tumults
of stormily-rapturous feeling, and suddenly, separate,
mirrors, drawing up their own
outstreamed beauty into their faces again.

The paradox of Konarak and, I believe, its poetry and beauty, have their source in the fact that these lavishly carved idols are carried to the furthest possible limit of the visible. Even the sculptor who carved the green chlorite sun god wrestles with the paradox of near-invisible effulgence within the restricting conventions of a style. The motivation for this Orissan extravagance of imagery is not wholly or even mainly erotic. I believe it is born of integral perception. Sūrya worship itself is pushed to the furthest limits by the Oriya people, inasmuch as the cult of the sun god has been transmitted into the cult of Dharma, the Universal Order, whose symbol is the *Dharmachakra*, one single wheel. The folk still attest to the truth of a statement by invoking the Sūrya form of Dharma, the irreversible ordinance in the Cosmos as well as in the life of individuals. Dharma was worshipped in the workmen's common room at Konarak as a lumpish, formless, white stone. One branch of the cult, the Dharma Pūjā Vidhana, prescribes the following meditation: 'Dharma is luminous like the Sun, it has the circular shape of Zero like the Sun, it moves in the Void like the Sun, and is, like the Sun, the origin or cause of creation, preservation and dissolution.' It may seem strange to associate this reaching beyond form to a Formless Beyond with so unabashed a celebration of the delights of the flesh. But that is the whole point, or rather it seems to me to evoke the very essence of sexual experience, which strains the limits, too, of language. The Indian is arguably the most consistently idolatrous of his species, even to the point of striving after a form which can adequately contain this supremely volatile experience.

A French philosopher of art, Elie Faure, is one of the only thinkers who has a good word to say for idolatry. In *The Spirit of the Forms*, he was of the firm opinion that the 'greatest moments of the spirit are those of idolatry, because from each we get one of the aspects of the definitive idol which we shall never carve. . . . Thereupon the spirit seeks elsewhere, it reaches some spot where there is no longer any visible form, and finally adores itself in its immaterial essence until the day when, turning to emptiness, consumed by its passion,

Sūrya Temple, Konarak

Wildman and his lover. Sūrya
Temple, Konarak

it seizes from the hot ashes of itself certain hard nuclei, veined with
fire, in which it gradually perceives new appearances. The soul of
mankind does not increase itself, or at least does not find itself again,
unless the matter of mankind transmit to it, through the contact of
the senses with the matter of the universe, the soul of that matter, in
which man's soul recognizes itself. What man adores in the idol is in
no wise outside himself, neither is it in any wise outside the world
of the senses, which is so made as to reveal to him his own sensibility. It incarnates his spiritual life in its ever-fleeting form. In it
he seizes his power of renewing his qualities.'

Indians who seek some immaterial essence both within the self and in the universe are traditionally the Wild Man, the poet, the sadhu, and the holy wanderer. These people have no temples, eschew ritual, and express their ideal of sahaja through the parabolic language of song. Now it is interesting that there are several very prominent and spirited portrayals of the Indian Wild Men at Konarak. They have been described as 'ascetics', but this is patently absurd; they are as deeply involved as everyone else in amorous love-play. While they wear their hair long and are of wild demeanour, they are not gross or ridiculous, like the ascetics of Khajuraho and elsewhere. On the contrary, they are splendid, beautiful and virile.

One of the real Wild Men of this period was a Sahajin bard by the name of Śavara-pāda, a 'barbarian', a 'savage', a 'mountaineer wearing peacock feathers'. He sings in the allusive style of all such songs: 'High is the mountain [the spinal column as experienced in yoga, channel of the female serpent power] and there in the highest chakra sits the Śavarī girl, decorated with peacock feathers and wearing flower garlands on her neck. O entranced, mad Śavara [exclaims the girl] do not revel in worldly pleasures, I am thy beloved consort, Sahaja Sundarī. On the mountain, many are the trees whose branches touch the sky – the Śavarī girl, wearing earrings and holding the thunder, plays alone in the forest.' In another song Śavara-pāda says: 'The bedstead of the three elements [body, speech and mind] is placed, and the serpent-like Śavara and the goddess Nairāmanī pass their night of love on that bed in great bliss.' This is the *unio mystica* as celebrated in a song which springs from folk culture. The Wild Man of Konarak may be a quasi-mythical figure of folklore, but he is close kin to a figure common in real life, and very much alive even in modern India. The most extraordinary of such eccentrics belong to the centuries-old Bengali order of wandering minstrels, the Bauls. These men are to medieval and modern Bengal what the Wild Man, or Wood-wose, is to European folklore. Having spent many days in the company of a celebrated member of this extraordinary sect, and sat with his wife and son in Bhirbum, listening to his songs by the moonlit fire, I can attest to the warmth and lyrical spirituality of the Bauls. Das Gupta has translated very freely this appreciative description of the Baul Wild Man from one of their songs:

Reverse are the modes and manners of the man who is a real appreciator of the true emotional life and who is a lover of true love; none is sure about the how and the when of his behaviour.

Such a man is affected neither by the weal nor by the woe of the world, and constantly realizes the delight of love; it appears that his eyes are floating on the water of delight; sometimes he laughs alone in his own mood, sometimes he cries alone.

He lights the lamp of love and sits on and on with his mind immersed in the fathomless depth of the sea of emotion; he has in his hand the key for happiness, but he never seeks it.

Awkwardly wild are all his manners and customs – and the other extremely wonderful fact is that the glory of the full-moon closes round him for all time; and further, this moon ceases not to shine day and night – there is no setting of the moon of his heart. . . .

My friend and travelling companion in Bengal, Deben Bhattacharya, has translated some Baul songs in *The Mirror of the Sky*. One of the modern songs typifies the way such people seek a more harmonious inner balance to their sexuality in the *unio mystica*:

> My heart,
> Dress yourself
> In the spirit of all women
> And reverse
> Your nature
> And habits . . .
>
> Millions of suns
> Will burst open
> With brilliance,
> And the formless
> In visual forms.
> You will see
> What cannot be seen
> Only if you can be
> The formless
> In you . . .

I have mentioned the Wild Man of European folklore alongside the real contemporary Wild Man of India so that each tradition may become porous to the other in the reader's mind. This way, perhaps, we may reach a closer, inner understanding of the lyrical feeling which informs this final masterpiece of India's erotic temple sculptures at Konarak.

I would like to end by quoting from two poems, the first from the *Jnāna-sāgar* of Aliraja, as transcribed by Das Gupta, the second by one of the greatest lyrical poets of this century, Rilke. Each illuminates the hidden meaning of those stones at Konarak, carved with the eye of Love.

It is said . . . that the universe has its origin in love, and the chaos is systematized into the cosmos through the bond of love. There is love between fire and air, between earth and water; without this love neither heaven, nor earth, nor the nether world would have originated at all. There is love between heaven and the skies, between heaven and earth, between hell and the nether world in which it lies, and thus are the three worlds supported in love. There is love between the sun, the moon, the planets and the stars and in love they are all fixed into the sky above. There is love between the sea and its water, between the moon and the night and the sun and the day; – the tree is fixed to the earth by its root, the black bee is attached to the lotus, fish is bound to the water, man is bound to the woman – and all in love. The body is in love with the mind and the mind with the vital wind. In love does the mother conceive the child, in love does the earth hold fast the root of the tree, in love does the tree hold fast the branches and the flowers and fruits, in love does the fruit accumulate juice in its kernel – thus is the whole creative process supported in love.

> Lovers, to you, each satisfied in the other,
> I turn with my question about us. You grasp yourselves.
>   Have you proofs?
> Look, with me it may happen at times that my hands
> grow aware of each other, or else that my hard-worn face
> seeks refuge within them. That gives me a little
> sensation. But who, just for that, could presume to exist?
> You, though, that go on growing
> in the other's rapture till, overwhelming, he implored
> 'No more'; you that under each other's hands
> grow more abundant like vintage grapes;
> swooning at times, just because the other
> has so expanded: I ask you about us. I know
> why you so blissfully touch: because the caress witholds,
> because it does not vanish, the place that you
> so tenderly cover; because you perceive thereunder
> pure duration. Until your embraces almost
> promise eternity.

OVERLEAF : *Konarak. Sūrya*
Temple from the south.

Bibliography

Mulk Raj Anand, *Kama Kala*, Nagel, Geneva, 1958.

Georges Bataille, *Eroticism*, Mary Dalwood (tr.), John Calder, London, 1962.

Agehananda Bharati, *The Ochre Robe*, George Allen and Unwin, London, 1961.

Deben Bhattacharya, *The Mirror of the Sky: songs of the Bauls from Bengal*, George Allen and Unwin, London, 1969.

Alice Boner and Sadasiva Rath Sarma, tr. and notes on *Silpa Prakasa*, by Ramachandra Kaulachara, E. J. Brill, Leiden, 1966.

—— and Sarma-Das, *New Light on the Sun Temple*, Varanasi, 1973.

S. B. Das Gupta, *Obscure Religious Cults*, Firma K. L. Mukhopadhyay, 3rd ed., Calcutta, 1969.

Devangana Desai, *Erotic Sculpture of India: a socio-cultural study*, Tata McGraw-Hill, New Delhi, 1975.

Mircea Éliade, *Yoga: Immortality and Freedom*, W. R. Trask (tr.), Routledge and Kegan Paul, London, 1964; Bollingen Series LXXVI, Pantheon Books, New York, 1958.

Verrier Elwin, *The Kingdom of the Young*, Oxford University Press, Bombay, 1968.

Élie Faure, *History of Art*, Vol. V: *The Spirit of the Forms*, W. Pach (tr.), John Lane, The Bodley Head, London, 1930.

Marcel Flory, *Les Temples de Khajuraho*, Delpire, Paris, 1965.

Max-Pol Fouchet, *The Erotic Sculpture of India*, George Allen and Unwin, London, 1959; S. G. Phillips, New York, 1959.

O. C. Gangoly, *Konarak*, Calcutta, 1956.

Jayadeva, *Gitagovinda*, George Keyt (tr.), Kutub Publishers, Bombay, 1947.

Koka Shastra, Alex Comfort (tr.), Preface by W. G. Archer, George Allen and Unwin, 1964.

Stella Kramrisch, *The Hindu Temple*, 2 vols., University of Calcutta Press, 1964.

K. Lal, *Immortal Khajuraho*, Asia Press, Delhi, 1965.

Richard Lannoy, *The Speaking Tree: a study of Indian culture and society*, Oxford University Press, London, New York, 1971.

Curt Maury, *Folk Origins of Indian Art*, Columbia University Press, New York and London, 1969.

Ajit Mookerjee, *Tantra Art: its philosophy and physics*, Ravi Kumar, New Delhi, 1967.

— *Tantra Asana: a way to self-realisation*, Ravi Kumar, Basel, Paris, New Delhi, 1971.

— *Yoga Art*, Preface by Philip Rawson, Thames and Hudson, 1976.

Philip Rawson, *Erotic Art of the East*, Preface by Alex Comfort, New York, 1968.

Rainer Maria Rilke, *Selected Works*, Vol II, *Poetry*, J. B. Leishman (tr.), Hogarth Press, London, 1967.

Thomas Traherne, *Poems, Centuries and Three Thanksgivings*, Oxford University Press, London, New York, 1966.

Vātsyāyana, *The Kāma-Sūtra*, Sir Richard Burton and F. F. Arbuthnot (trs.), W. G. Archer (ed.), George Allen and Unwin, London, 1963.

Andreas Volwahsen, *Living Architecture: Indian*, Macdonald, London, 1969.

Alan Watts and Eliot Elisofon, *The Temple of Konarak: erotic spirituality*, Thames and Hudson, London, 1971.

Eliky Zannas and Jeannine Auboyer, *Khajuraho*, The Hague, 1960.